Won Over

ALSO BY WILLIAM ALSUP

Missing in the Minarets

Such a Landscape!

WON OVER

*Reflections of a Federal Judge on His
Journey from Jim Crow Mississippi*

WILLIAM ALSUP

FOREWORD BY THELTON HENDERSON

NEWSOUTH BOOKS
Montgomery

NewSouth Books
105 S. Court Street
Montgomery, AL 36104

Library of Congress Cataloging-in-Publication Data

Names: Alsup, William H., author.
Title: Won over: reflections of a federal judge on his journey from jim crow
Mississippi / William Alsup.

Description: Montgomery, AL : NewSouth Books, [2019].
Identifiers: LCCN 2018031632 | ISBN 9781588383426 (hardcover)
Subjects: LCSH: Alsup, William H.—Childhood and youth. | Civil rights workers—
Mississippi—Biography. | Mississippi—Race relations—History—20th century. |
University of Mississippi—Students—Biography. | Law students—Mississippi—
Biography.| Youth, White—Mississippi—Biography. | Cupit, Danny—Childhood
and youth. | Civil rights movements—Mississippi—History—20th century. |
Racism—Mississippi. | Jackson (Miss.)—Biography.
Classification: LCC F345.3.A47 A3 2019 | DDC 323.092 [B] —dc23
LC record available at https://lccn.loc.gov/2018031632

Printed in the United States of America

For Willanna

Contents

Foreword / IX

Acknowledgments / XII

Looking Back / 3

1   The Billboard / 4

2   Mississippi / 8

3   The Mississippi Way of Life / 18

4   Separate But Equal All Over Again / 30

5   Catastrophe / 31

6   Pals / 34

7   The Right of Protest / 41

8   Blowing in the Wind / 45

9   Camelot and Cuba / 48

10   James Meredith at Ole Miss / 53

11   Utterly Empty / 59

12   Cool Like the Kennedys / 61

13   A Ride on the Rails / 67

14   That Word / 69

15   'We Are for Civil Rights for Negroes' / 70

16   The Murder of Medgar Evers / 78

17   Class Reunion / 81

18   The Summer of 1963 / 82

19   A Dinner at Lalime's / 87

20   Get an Education—the Ticket to Somewhere / 88

21   MSU Debate / 96

22   A Blood-Soaked Miracle: The Civil Rights Act of 1964 / 100

23 Danny Cupit / 110

24 Our Condolences to Charles Evers / 112

25 Another Miracle: The Voting Rights Act of 1965 / 115

26 National Contenders / 117

27 The Coolest Place on Campus / 122

28 Setting the Stage / 126

29 Inspired by Bobby / 135

30 The Meredith March and Dr. King / 142

31 Katrina / 155

32 A Stand Against Evil / 157

33 The First Black Speaker on a White Campus in Mississippi / 170

34 Reprisals / 176

35 Riding the Wind / 180

36 A Tank Commander / 181

37 More Assassinations / 183

38 Danny Brings the First Amendment to Mississippi / 185

39 Back Home in Mississippi / 187

40 Mississippi in the Sierra / 191

41 Willanna / 193

42 What Became of Us / 195

43 Conclusion / 201

Foreword

The Honorable Thelton Henderson

For the past thirty-seven years, a frame in my chambers has displayed a now-faded leaflet posing this question in bold letters:

WHAT HAVE I PERSONALLY DONE
TO MAINTAIN SEGREGATION?

I came upon this flyer in 1963 in a doctor's office in Selma, Alabama, but it could just as well have been from Jackson, Mississippi, the hometown of William Alsup. Bill was born there at the end of the war. He grew up in Mississippi. His parents and nearly everyone white around him favored segregation. Bill, too, would've headed down that path, but, step by step during the zenith of the civil rights movement, he was won over to the right side of history.

Rather than ask what he had personally done to maintain segregation, Bill questioned whether it was right that black kids were treated differently and that people of different races could not pray together. He wondered how African American schoolchildren in Little Rock, Arkansas, must have felt as they integrated schools, escorted by the 101st Airborne Division, and walked into the venom of shrieking whites. He watched as the Freedom Riders came to his hometown, then got slammed into jail as if criminals. He witnessed the cruelty of racism, both on television and in the streets, and eventually realized how wrong it was. As his high school years ended in June 1963, Bill and a few close friends found the courage to speak out publicly in favor of voting rights for African Americans. On their behalf, he wrote a letter to the editor of the *Clarion-Ledger*, the dominant newspaper in Mississippi. That letter, published on June 6, 1963, declared, "We are for civil rights for Negroes."

Then, in 1966, as a student at Mississippi State University, Bill walked door to door to encourage voter registration in the African American community and fought his university's administration in a high-profile contest over whether the president of the Mississippi NAACP would be allowed to speak on campus. Bill and his colleagues won that battle. In January 1967, they witnessed the first black guest ever to give a speech on a traditionally white campus. And they helped welcome Richard Holmes, Mississippi State's first African American student. None of these actions were popular back then, but a few white students did them anyway—because they were right and just.

What caused that young white boy in the "closed society" of Mississippi to take the less-traveled path? An older sister who saw through the system? A close pal who admired Lincoln? Faculty mentors with conscience and courage? A roommate who saw where America was headed and joined the movement? Parents who though segregationists believed that all of God's children should be able to worship together at any house of God? Seeing the injustice with his own eyes? Sitting in a black church with Dr. Martin Luther King Jr. in the pulpit?

This memoir charts the course, through its zigzags and missteps, that called him.

Unbeknownst to either of us in 1963, Bill and I were both fighting battles in the same war for equal rights. Me—a black government lawyer born in Louisiana but raised in California—from the outside. Bill—a white Mississippian—from the inside. In 1963, both of us were in Jackson, but our paths didn't cross until decades later.

Fast forward to 1998—I am now a judge on the United States District Court in San Francisco. Having turned sixty-five after more than fifteen years on the federal bench, I am eligible to take senior status and decide to do so. This allows me to continue to serve as a judge while freeing a seat on the bench for the President, with the advice and consent of the Senate, to fill. In early 1999, President Bill Clinton appoints Bill, by now a seasoned trial lawyer in San Francisco, to take my position on the court. The Senate confirms his appointment.

When Bill was formally inducted into our Court on January 27, 2000, I said that it would not be possible for me to be prouder or more pleased that Bill was taking my seat on the bench. But I was wrong. Having gotten to know Bill well over our nearly two decades as colleagues, I am, in fact, now more proud and pleased than ever.

Although we both worked to promote racial equality in the sixties (and beyond), our experiences differed—in part because of the different colors of our skin. Yet, as I have learned through countless conversations with Bill over the years, we share many of the same core values. Among those is the desire to live in a world where "equality under the law" is not just a motto but a reality, and where society treats everyone not just equally, but equitably. While racial and social divides are once again boiling to the surface, I cannot help but think that this memoir will remind us of important influences, some serendipitous, that can reroute and redirect our youth along the arc of justice.

The Honorable Thelton Henderson is a United
States District Judge in San Francisco
(2002, photograph by the author)

Acknowledgments

For critiquing drafts of this work, I acknowledge and thank my sisters Willanna and Sandy, and our daughter, Allison, along with: Junior Feild, Joe Turnage, Ron Goodbread, Walter Dowdle, Sidney Craft, Ann Smith Willoughby, Leslie Westbrook, and Danny Cupit, all friends since Provine High School (or earlier); Kirk Shaw, Brad Bishop, Cermette Clardy, Susan Eiland Rickman, Debbie Davis Rabinowitz, and Camilla Wilson, friends and mentors at Mississippi State; Ryan Semmes, associate professor and coordinator of the Congressional and Political Research Center, Sara Frederick, director of development, College of Arts and Sciences, both now at Mississippi State; Peter Pfister and Mel Goldman, former law partners in San Francisco; Judges Martin Jenkins and Thelton Henderson, colleagues on our federal district court; Jim and Joe Garrett, two faithful hiking pals, John Hendricks, formerly a librarian for our court; Sylvia Zaich, my former extern from the University of Southern California; Beth Marino and Randall Williams, editors superb at NewSouth Books; and, most of all, Katherine Young, my ever loyal secretary and true friend.

Kathy came to work as my secretary in 1985. She began life in China and immigrated with her family in 1959. They lived in Birmingham when she was young. Her uncle ran the Joy Young Chinese food restaurant in Birmingham, one of Brad's favorites (and my first experience in a Chinese restaurant). Then they moved to San Francisco. After high school Kathy launched a career as a secretary—and she proved to be a most excellent one. She stayed with me when I came to the district court and is with me yet. "Stellar" understates her ability to turn out letter-perfect briefs (and now orders) in record time and to manage our chambers like Mother Hen. She typed every draft of this manuscript. I remain very obliged to her.

Won Over

Looking Back

In a race-discrimination lawsuit here in our federal district court in San Francisco, I am obliged under the law to rule against the plaintiff, an African American. His lawyer then seeks to disqualify me as the judge on the ground that, as a white man born and raised in Mississippi, I must have deep-seated residual racism. He argues, "You can go to Harvard, and you can clerk for Justice Douglas, but old institutionalized race and class attitudes are deeply ingrained early."

The year is 2011.

Another district judge rules on the motion to disqualify and denies it, so I continue on the case. Now the plaintiff's lawyer asks me to recuse myself on the same ground, that my Mississippi roots make me incapable of issuing a fair ruling in this case. Putting aside the sting of the accusation, I understand where the lawyer is coming from. Both of us are old enough to remember the fifties and sixties. In the quiet of my chambers in San Francisco, I pause to reflect on my youth in Mississippi, the tumult of the civil rights movement, and how those years affected my attitudes on the monumental issues of race and equal justice. The right thing to do is to deny the lawyer's request. Growing up white in Mississippi, I say in a brief ruling, opened, not closed, my eyes to the cruelty of racism.

1

The Billboard

W e'd only heard about it, so my best pal Ron and I drove out to see it. Sure enough, in towering letters beside an image of an American flag, the billboard called for the removal of the Chief Justice of the United States. "Impeach Earl Warren," it blared, beneath a banner imploring "Save Our Republic." The billboard stood on a rise along U.S. Highway 80, just west of our hometown, Jackson. The John Birch Society sponsored the sign, along with others like it all over the country. The billboard captured the sentiment of most of white Mississippi, which blamed Earl Warren for the Supreme Court's decision in *Brown v. Board of Education*, the 1954 school desegregation case. Warren had delivered the unanimous ruling, which declared that "separate but equal" had no place in public education. Most white Mississippians hated the entire federal government, not just Warren. Most of all, they hated the Kennedys.

The calendar read February 6, 1963.

We were seventeen, seniors in high school.

Ron fumed over the billboard. Tall, skinny, and from humble roots like his hero, Abe Lincoln, Ron had already read more history than most college graduates. He'd mastered, for example, Carl Sandburg's six-volume work on Lincoln. For Ron, the federal government exemplified Lincoln and his sacrifice, so the billboard infuriated him.

"Those right-wing bastards" was how he liked to begin his smart-ass commentaries on Mississippi politics. For my part, not being so well-read (but nevertheless a smart-ass), I took my history from Ron, a storyteller

4

without equal in our crowd. Ron thought we owed respect to the Chief Justice, so it rubbed off a little. I tried to feel the same way.

As we took in the billboard, we got so worked up that we decided to go out that night to paint over the "Impeach Earl Warren" part, provided we could find enough leftover house paint. Our plot led to my garage, where we found enough to fill two cans. It mixed together as beige. We put the two cans, along with my dad's Army machete, in the trunk of my mom's 1954 Chrysler sedan.

As we waited for darkness, I dialed Ann. A tall, vivacious brunette, Ann Smith had asked me to tutor her in algebra. I'd leapt at the chance. This led to some innocent dates, including a perfect picnic along the trenches of the Vicksburg campaign. We weren't an item, though. I settled for her friendship, too shy to angle for more.

I told Ann our plan.

"That's great," she said. "Can I come, too?"

I'd hoped she'd be impressed—but going along? That had never occurred to me.

"Okay," I replied, trying to stay cool, "we'll pick you up on the way out there."

I was stuck. Entertaining doubts all along, I'd mainly been talking big, figuring a convenient excuse could always be invented to back out. Now I had to go through with it. Ron, who was unrepentantly contemptuous of the system, never had any doubts. He couldn't wait for sundown.

I drove. We picked up Ann and headed over to Highway 80. The illuminated billboard shone against the evening sky. We spotted a lonely dirt lane running behind the sign. Turning off the highway, we crept down the dark lane, pulling over so the car was out of sight of the highway. We hadn't done anything irreversible yet, but my voice got tight with nerves.

"We better turn around, so we'll be headed the right way," I strained. "We may have to get the hell out of here." At least I could still think.

"I can't wait to see the headline," Ron crowed. "Those bastards."

"This is so great," Ann laughed. "You two are something else."

We turned off the headlights, got out, then retrieved the paint and the machete. The moon was a little before full, so the deserted lane remained

Ann Smith, about the time of the billboard protest (1963)

shadowy. I insisted that Ann stay with the car. Ron and I headed for the billboard, single-file, commando-like, threading through the pines and brush. There!—Shining through the woods we saw it. No fences. No obstacles. Amazingly easy to reach. Arriving at the billboard, we heard, then saw, cars whizzing on the highway below the rise.

We swung into action.

Whack!—I lopped off a large pine branch with the machete.

Now we had a huge paint brush. We stowed it in front of the sign, then took the two paint cans around to the rear of the billboard. Ron scrambled up to the bottom horizontal support, and I handed him the paint. I leap-frogged above him to the middle support, then he handed me the cans. He scrambled to the top support, and the cans followed. I jumped down to run around to the front. Up there loomed Ron, leaning over the top of the billboard. I aligned him right above the offending phrase. (We wanted to avoid smearing the flag.)

"You ready?" he asked.

I stood, poised with our paint brush.

"Go ahead," I answered.

He poured a can of paint down the sign while I swept the thick beige paint back and forth with the long branch.

We imagined travelers on the highway below us exclaiming, "God

Almighty, look, some assholes are up there painting the 'Impeach Earl Warren' sign."

"We need the second can," I called up to Ron.

Down it oozed. More smearing.

Ron leapt down. I tossed the limb aside.

We hurried back to the car, not even pausing to admire our handiwork, tossed our machete and paint cans into the trunk, then got the hell out of there. Just after we got back on the highway, we saw several Mississippi Highway Patrol cruisers converging on the scene.

Our work became a big item on the next day's local television news. The *Jackson Daily News* ran a photograph of the defaced sign captioned, "Vandals Smear Billboard." The local president of the John Birch Society made hay, saying the smear job proved that "communists, socialists, internationalists and one-worlders" lurked right there in Jackson. What was a "one-worlder"? Ann and I worried. Ron did not. He loved it and snorted with contempt at the entire regime.

Mother eventually asked, "Son, did you paint up that sign?"

I couldn't lie to her.

"Yes," I replied.

"Well, son, you better be careful."

That was all she ever said.

Had my dad still been alive, I never would have done it in the first place. He would have severely disapproved. It would only have confirmed his worst suspicions about "Long Hair," as he called Ron, with his Elvis pompadour.

It blew over.

We had no idea that we'd taken a step in a journey, one that would culminate in a handful of homegrown white kids finding the courage to very publicly take on Jim Crow.

2

Mississippi

Mississippi is a word loaded with harsh meaning in American history, but Mississippi is also a place, a beautiful place. Most of its western border is etched by the Father of Waters, the Mississippi River. Its southern reach lies at a magnificent white-sand beach along the Gulf Coast. Tennessee, Louisiana, and Alabama supply its other borders. In between spread millions of pines mixed with hardwoods, as well as farms and ranches across a landscape broken by muddy waterways, often decorated with kudzu vines and Spanish moss. One small mountain rises to 806 feet, the highest point in the state. The coastal plain (the southeast quadrant of the state) and the Delta (the northwest quadrant) are flatness quintessential. In the undulating country of the northeast quadrant, we find Mississippi State University, the stage of so much of this story, over near the Alabama line. The capital of Mississippi is Jackson, named for the soldier-president, and it sits at about the dead center of the state, at the crossroads of U.S. Highways 80 and 51.

Jackson is where our story begins, in 1940.

There, newly arrived from Texas, our parents spent their last ten cents on a watermelon. Pregnant with their first child, Mother craved watermelon, so that dime went for one. Then they were broke. Worse, they were broke in a strange new land. It seemed odd that they had come looking for work to Mississippi, a place that ranked as the poorest of the poor, a place that had barely improved its standard of living since Reconstruction. Horse-drawn wagons still rattled along roadways. In those first few months, my mother marveled over (and kept) a photograph of two black women walking on a country road, balancing large bundles on their heads, a scene that might have been observed at least a century earlier.

The Great Depression still gripped our nation. America's part in the Second World War seemed only an ominous thunderhead looming on the horizon. Jobs remained scarce. Dad had learned surveying and the basics of civil engineering in West Texas working for the Work Projects Administration—the WPA. In Jackson, engineer William Mallett gave him work. Out of gratitude, when their firstborn came along near Christmas 1940, my parents named her after Mr. Mallett's wife, Willanna, a wonderful lady who took a lasting interest in her namesake.

Then came Pearl Harbor. Dad went into the Army Corps of Engineers, then to North Africa in the 344th Engineer General Services Regiment. Mother had trained as a nurse but suspended her practice when they came to Mississippi. During the war, Willanna and Mother lived with relatives in Texas. Our dad returned home to Jackson in 1944, medically discharged. He mustered out as a captain. I came along in June 1945. Sandy joined us two years later.

A photograph Mother kept of a Mississippi scene (1940)

Mother was Jewel Emma, and Dad was William Haskell, born in 1913 and 1909, respectively. They stood tall, thin with dark graying hair. He had pale blue eyes; she had brown eyes. His looked out from behind wire-frame bifocals, often peering into a toolbox, hers from behind black cat-eye reading glasses, often hovering over a crossword puzzle. Both practiced economy with words. She had a contagious, lilting laugh. He was all business—sometimes with a temper.

Dad acquired a veteran's preference for lumber in the immediate aftermath of the war, so in 1948 ours became one of the first postwar new homes in Jackson. I was a toddler when we moved into a one-story white frame house at 2325 Terry Road, just inside the city limits on the south side of town, then just sixty thousand residents. It featured two small bedrooms, one bath, a kitchen, a combination living plus dining room, a screened porch, and a one-car garage. Annexed to the rear of the garage was a "wash house" for our washing machine, an antique with a handcranked wringer to squeeze out water, but sometimes we still washed clothes in a washtub with a washboard in the backyard. We never had a dryer—just three clotheslines. Nor did we ever have central heating or cooling—just an attic fan that drew air in through the open windows and pushed it out through the attic. Terry Road doubled as U.S. Highway 51, a two-lane ribbon between Chicago and New Orleans. Four huge oak trees soared on our front yard along the highway. Between the first two ran our gravel-on-dirt driveway.

Next door lived a farmer and his wife, Ernest and Edna Brown, on a fifteen-acre parcel complete with barn. Across Terry Road from us stood a one-room cinderblock general store known as Nell's Grocery. Otherwise, we were surrounded by endless fields, creeks, and woods.

In our large side and back yards we grew corn, grapes, tomatoes, okra, green beans, and lima beans. We raised chickens and collected fresh eggs until the early 1950s. In the spring, Murray, a black man known to us kids only by his first name, drove his wagon to our house, unhitched his mule, hitched it to a plow, harnessed himself in tow, then turned true furrows across our side field of about one acre. Our family then planted rows with seed corn, we wide-eyed youngsters checking each morning to see how many seedlings had popped through the dirt.

Above, our home on Terry Road in south Jackson and Mother's Chrysler (1963); below, Mother at "Andy's Tree" (1966)

We kids had brown eyes and brown hair. With freckles galore, smart and bossy, a natural artist, Willanna was the eldest. Sandy, the youngest, was quiet, kind, and compliant. She had a strong affinity for animals, regularly acquiring no end of cats and assorted pets. Sandy had a twin brother, Andrew, who lived only four days. In his memory, we planted "Andy's Tree," a mimosa, in the middle of our backyard next to the clotheslines. Sandwiched between my sisters, I began life as a curious, mischievous, and pudgy toddler but eventually turned into a tall, skinny, cheeky teenager. Our registered collie was officially "Will's Reward," but our dad called every dog "Hound Dog," so that name stuck. Hound Dog would eventually save his life.

The fifties became a period of renewed hope, a period casting off the Great Depression and luxuriating in the afterglow of our victory in the Second World War. As postwar expansion in the early 1950s crept even into obscure places like Jackson, the woods behind us gave way slowly to new homes on a dirt road, later paved. Civilization! So, we gradually gave up farm life to convert our yard to grass, shrubs, grapes, and fruit trees—always suspecting that our new subdivision neighbors regarded us yet as country folk. In the mid-1950s, Dad bought a second car for the family. He added a carport on one end of the house, then, on the other, another bedroom with a bath for Sandy and Willanna.

Schoolwork dominated most of my childhood. Besides that, I mowed our acre-plus land and helped our dad with chores, sometimes getting fifty cents for doing it. I had a *State Times* paper route and loved to ride my bike (always secondhand). I shot my BB gun, explored the woods, swam, climbed trees, swung on vines, flew kites, teased Sandy, obeyed Willanna, adored Pop (Dad's father from Texas, who visited each summer), took dancing lessons, tried to teach myself the piano, wore a Cub Scout uniform, earned an amateur radio license (WA5EG1, later N6XMW), served as a street-crossing guard, played chase with our collie, collected army patches, airplane cards, marbles, stamps, and coins, and spent innumerable days and nights with pals introduced below. Most of every summer I went barefoot. The rest of the year I had one pair of sneakers plus one pair of Sunday shoes. After Sputnik in 1957, we lay in the grass to watch the night sky for satellites and UFOs. Yes, of course, we chased fireflies. Willanna gave me a five-year diary and told me to make entries daily, so I did, until midway through college when I switched to a journal (with fewer but longer entries). I attended church, invariably saying a prayer for our dad and his health.

Here's what I didn't do—other than science and math, I didn't read very much. My adult years have been consumed by reading, mostly American history, but back then I read as little as possible. Literature and history didn't rate. Nor did I become much of a ladies' man, being shy in that department. Although in later life black-and-white film photography became a passion, I had no camera then. Nor did I smoke, drink, or use substances—boring,

Willanna and me in our cornfield (1948)

but true. Going out for meals came with blue moons; we regularly ate around our small kitchen table. One hand could count the few times our family went out to eat in Jackson. I was no good at sports and barely even made a Little League team, though my pals and I loved sandlot football and baseball. Computers, the Internet, and cell phones were still off in a distant, unseen future and would have seemed like something out of Dick Tracy.

In our dining room we had a wooden cabinet radio. I used to peer through its crevices at the glowing tubes inside, seeking the origin of the music, imagining tiny performers within. When I was seven, we upgraded. Dad brought home a black-and-white tube television, also housed in a cabinet. He climbed onto the roof to raise an antenna. After much profanity—profanity always facilitated such household projects—we got our first pictures. They showed American warships heading to the Korean War, soon followed by the coronation of Queen Elizabeth, all via Channel 12, WJTV, a CBS affiliate, the only station then serving Jackson. By high school, we regularly lived for the next episode of *The Twilight Zone* by Rod Serling and the *Falstaff Game of the Week* announced by baseball greats Dizzy Dean and Pee Wee Reese, all on that black-and-white television.

By parental fiat, Sandy and I attended a nearby Presbyterian church and its Sunday school. Willanna somehow got exempted or maybe just refused to go. When she was in high school, she studied evolution (on her own), then decided that the Book of Genesis had it all wrong. For me, however, organized religion became a regular part of my life. My diary collected a lot of references to the Bible, at least through my early college years. Later on, during college, I came to believe what I now think Abraham Lincoln believed—there must be an Almighty, but virtue should be its own reward—we need not belong to any organized religion to do good. Willanna, I eventually concluded, proved right about evolution.

Our parents and Willanna (almost five years my senior) predominated as the primary influences for Sandy and me. They emphasized schoolwork. We got a dime for each A on a report card. Willanna operated her own kindergarten on the screened porch for us, appointing herself the teacher—she was a good one too. From our parents, we heard about the Great Depression and the tremendous value of an education. Through them, we came to respect hard, honest work and to see the American work ethic as one of our nation's greatest strengths.

Our dad's work was power line construction. With his partner he ran "Gulfport Construction Company." He even had a pilot's license and flew the lines under construction, sometimes taking me along for a ride. The early 1950s proved to be the salad days for his business. In a good year he cleared $5,000, then about three times the median income in Mississippi, the poorest state in the Union. His strength was good engineering judgment, especially in the field. He could make crisp, sound decisions. He got the job done on time and on budget. Through the late 1950s, however, his health steadily worsened. Too often, he went into the hospital for one reason or another, mainly for diabetic seizures. His business suffered. His fading health cast an anxious pall over life at 2325 Terry Road. He became irritable but soldiered on in pain. Alcohol helped, all "bottled and bonded" under federal law yet illegal in dry Mississippi.

While our mom exuded gentleness, ever proud of her children, our dad exuded toughness, ever demanding more. In my incorrigible early teenage years, he seemed fixated on two maxims. One: "I hate a liar worse than a thief." The truth was, I rarely lied to him and never stole from him. The other: "You'd better straighten up and fly right." This one had more purchase. It came up frequently, for he often had to ask me twice to mow the grass, which grew like crazy in that subtropical clime, or to complete some other household chore. Eventually I did them, but it aggravated him that he even had to ask at all. Worse, I would pull dumb stunts, like the time I rode in the back seat of his car, lit a firecracker, then tossed it out the window, only to have it blow back in at sixty miles an hour to explode inside the car. Dad was not amused.

But he had a soft side, too. Once, unbeknownst to anyone else, he went with the dog alone out in the country, where he waded into a remote pond to retrieve a rowboat. Dad slipped into an underwater hole left by a removed tree trunk. He could not squirm out. Fortunately, his head stayed above water, but how long could he keep standing? He called our collie who, sensing trouble, swam out to him. Dad used Hound Dog's momentum as leverage to pull himself free. I came home from school to see him grilling a steak and asked why we were eating so early. He replied, "It's not for us. It's for the dog."

He sometimes showed his soft side to us kids. One spring, when I was five or so, he sat with me on the front porch, our feet in the cool grass with our butts on the concrete landing, admiring the new leaves on the tall oaks along the front.

"They're like your mother," he mused. "Every spring, they get a new dress."

He was enjoying a smoke. As we took in the moment, I asked him what smoking was like, so he gave me a puff. I gagged and rolled in the grass—so horrid a taste that I would never smoke again in my life. He did me a good turn that day.

Later, Dad would attend every Little League game. When I happened to do something worthwhile, which wasn't often, he would offer short praise like, "That was a good catch." Then, there was the time just after I got my driver's license and was leaving on my first-ever date that he slipped me an extra five dollars, told me to have a good time, then gave me a sly look.

As was common among Second World War veterans, he rarely talked about his service. One of his Army buddies also lived in Jackson. They'd served together in North Africa. Our two families socialized every few months in one backyard or another. Even then, though, our two veterans said little about their Army years.

My dad, I later discovered, had kept a journal during the war (as well as during his WPA days in the 1930s). That journal traced his doings, fears, and dreams more intimately than he ever had done while alive. It told, for example, how the German bombers flew over the American soldiers, night after night. On June 3, 1943, his journal entry read: "Jerry gave us hell last nite and bombed a fort and covered up 150 French soldiers—we are digging them out—3 alive so far—many dead." Some of his entries were written to "My Darlings," referring to Mother and Willanna, then a toddler. On February 2, 1943, he used his flashlight to write an entry for the two of them, telling Willanna that the pup tent would be "large enough for a playhouse," then telling Mother, "I'd love to share it with you."

In a dusty, hot loft in the garage was a wooden footlocker. It had been made by his unit in North Africa as a gift when he came back to the

United States—very ill. I would sneak up there sometimes to admire the contents—his uniform, his combat belt, an Army-issue machete in a khaki canvas sheath, some Algerian money, and miscellaneous other mementos of war. (His .45 Colt sidearm stayed locked up elsewhere.)

Once, in the backyard, while Dad was in an Adirondack chair enjoying a regular filterless Camel cigarette, his favorite, I asked him if he had ever killed anyone in the war. I was about six, and I hoped the answer would be yes. Without rising from the chair, he slapped me across the shoulder so hard I tumbled along the grass. A dumb question, I surmised. In time, it came to me: that had been his way of teaching me that life was precious, that killing someone, even in war, was awful, and that inquiring about it was extremely poor form. I remained proud, though, of that footlocker, the uniform, and all that they represented. America was a democracy. Hitler and Tojo had been tyrants. Democracy had gone to war with tyranny and had won unconditionally. Our dad had been part of the Greatest Army on Earth, part of that monumental achievement. Seventy more years have passed. Still, that pride burns bright.

Early one morning, just at sunrise, the phone rang. The timing meant bad news. I peeked through the vertical slit between the door and the jamb to see my dad, alone at our formica kitchen table, reaching back to his left for the Bakelite handset, then putting it to his ear. The little he said remained muted, all somber. He replaced the handset, lowered his head onto his forearms, then sobbed, his torso quaking. I had the good sense, for once, to remain quiet, to stay away. His own dad, Pop (whom we all adored), had just died in Texas. It was the only time I ever saw Dad in tears, this man who had seen war and death, who worked through pain without complaint every day. That was in August 1960.

By year end, he, too, would be dead.

3

The Mississippi Way of Life

Since before the Civil War, Mississippi has had more African Americans per capita than any other state, particularly concentrated in the counties along the Mississippi River. Prior to 1930, blacks outnumbered whites in Mississippi (and still do in many counties). In the sixties, they represented 42 percent of the statewide population. Yet the ruling class and mercantile class remained all-white. This system, which was standard throughout the South, with all the laws, customs, and mores that enforced it generally went by the euphemism "the Southern way of life," but closer to home, they called it "the Mississippi way of life."

My earliest memory that something was wrong traces back to an old schoolhouse. Our dad had acquired some fenced land south of Jackson where he kept thirty or so head of cattle. It was where Hound Dog saved his life. In the winters, when forage went scarce, we had to go down there to feed hay to our cattle. One day in the fifties, when I was about twelve, home sick from school, Dad took me with him to feed them. Cold rain drizzled along Terry Road. We spoke little. He smoked a Camel as he drove through the open country, his window cracked for ventilation. I stared out my rain-beaded window. We passed an old red sand quarry, where a large shanty rose on a puddled flat. I'd seen it many times before, but this time blue smoke curled from a woodstove pipe on a rusty tin roof, melding into the rain. A few grade school kids, all black, played outside a doorway in the red mud. I realized then that it was not an abandoned shack, as I had always thought, but a Negro school.

As the civil rights movement loomed larger, our parents remained mostly quiet on that subject. They usually kept their opinions to themselves. We were lucky there. We did not hear steady venomous talk about race as a few of my schoolmates did from their parents, hateful talk I overheard firsthand when visiting. So, we kids dodged serious indoctrination at home. Our parents were, in fact, conservative Texans who supported segregation—but they did not regularly preach it. They didn't belong to the Klan or the White Citizens' Council, or any other such group. (Nor, for that matter, did anyone we knew.) However, other Jim Crow customs prevailed, even in homes like ours. For example, all white children were taught to call black people, even adults, by their first name only, without ever even learning their last names. Yet we learned to call white adults by their last names, no matter how familiar they might be, as in "Mrs. Brown."

On our motor trips to Texas to see relatives, we crossed the Mississippi River. Coming back we usually had a family picnic in the national military park at Vicksburg, forty-two miles west of Jackson. Mother was always happy to arrive back in the Magnolia State, so a picnic became her way of recognizing the milestone. The Vicksburg park was all about the Civil War, so our talk sometimes turned to that conflict. Both parents told us that slavery had been wrong. Mother had been raised on a cotton farm near Waco, and along with all her many brothers and sisters, she planted, then picked, the annual cotton crop. Dad had been raised on a small Texas hill country farm farther west. Our parents understood the hard work enslaved people had once done better than we children did. Although they never put it in these terms, they essentially agreed with Lincoln that anyone who believed in slavery should try it on for size.

This did not mean they had doubts about segregation. To the contrary, a 1957 supper-time shouting match underscored that. Three years earlier the Supreme Court had ruled public school segregation unconstitutional in *Brown v. Board of Education*, overturning its 1896 "separate but equal" ruling in *Plessy v. Ferguson*. *Brown* had lit a firestorm. My sister Willanna, then in high school, decided she could and would be friends with anyone she wanted regardless of skin color—even a black. Willanna's view came out at the supper table. Our dad rarely said anything unless he "meant it." When he got upset, however, he could be volcanic. Now, he erupted, for socializing with Negroes was taboo. Willanna shouted back, holding her ground. He threatened to throw her out of the house. I was twelve and stunned by the intensity of their argument. What would Willanna do, I fretted, if she were turned out on the street? Where did she find the courage to stand up to our dad?

The Mississippi way of life certainly meant separate and unequal schools, libraries, and parks. And, it meant segregated and unequal neighborhoods, enforced via restrictive covenants. It also meant segregated seating on buses and trains and in courtrooms, even separate nights at the state fair. Some movie houses allowed seating for black people in the balcony.

How did segregation work in circumstances where the two races came together? On a typical Saturday morning, Capitol Street, the main thoroughfare in downtown Jackson, brimmed with traffic. Families came from all over central Mississippi to shop. The sidewalks throbbed with shoppers, both black and white—for merchants wanted everyone's money. On Capitol Street—near the dappled grounds of the antebellum governor's mansion—Jackson's two large, competing department stores, the Emporium and Kennington's, stood opposite each other. On the sidewalks out front and at the checkout lines, whites and blacks waited together in turn, usually extending common courtesies. The indignity of "Colored" and "White" water fountains came about precisely because the two races mixed in settings like department stores, public halls, and sidewalks.

Our department stores had dual water fountains but not dual dressing rooms because, as a strict rule, black shoppers were not allowed to try on clothing, let alone return it. For them, it was cash and carry without a right of return. Service stations never had a restroom for black customers, save for one or two "modern" stations in Jackson with a third bathroom for black customers—a single small room shared by men and women. Motels and hotels refused rooms to black guests. Downtown, we had no stores with two lunch counters, one for each race, like the one we would eventually see in New Orleans. We had only white lunch counters in Jackson. In some stores, black customers could be served via a takeout window in the rear. The bus station and the train station in Jackson had white waiting rooms and black waiting rooms, each with a lunch counter.

The Civil War felt as if it had just ended. A public park not two miles from our house was Battlefield Park (at the intersection of U.S. Highways 51 and 80). Union Generals Grant and Sherman had won that contest, a fact that usually came out only on careful cross-examination. White kids played war on the extensive Union earthworks then still in excellent condition. A little closer to home, a third of a mile away on Terry Road, an old home partially hidden in the woods had been used, it was said, by General Grant as a field headquarters and hospital—bloodstains supposedly were still visible on the floors. The general no doubt rode along Terry Road, passing our tall oaks in their youth. Throughout Mississippi, rebel flags flew. I myself had one in the fifties, along with fake Confederate bills, even a coonskin cap. As we grew up, the impression endured that the South had bravely stood up for self-determination in the Civil War and that in due course, in some vague unspecified way, the South would rise again.

In the Civil War, over six hundred thousand were killed out of a national population of thirty-one million, an enormous death toll, unmatched by any other American war. More Americans were killed in the Civil War than in all of the wars the United States has ever fought, from the Revolution to Iraq and Afghanistan, put together. The South, where most of the war was fought, suffered the most. White families ruined by the Union bayonet passed on their bitterness from generation to generation. In the 1950s and 1960s, the Civil War and its aftermath still felt vivid and recent, even as we celebrated the Civil War Centennial. White resentment lingered in the air like smoke after a forest fire.

Reconstruction had tried to set freed men and women on a road to full citizenship and participation in society. By 1876, however, that effort gave way to a national desire to heal the sectional wounds of the Civil War, which translated to a willingness to placate the South for the sake of reunification. The deep wounds and needs of formerly enslaved people then took a back seat to the desire of Southern white people to maintain the racial status quo. This led to a warped view of federalism, namely that the rest of the nation should simply mind its own business and let the South reconstruct itself, all under the banner of "states' rights." From 1876 until 1954, the federal government (and most of the nation) did exactly that, looking the other way, letting Mississippi, the South, indeed much of America, have their own way on race, meaning segregation with second-class status for non-whites. Jim Crow held sway. During that dark period, "separate but equal" remained the law of the land, enshrined in *Plessy v. Ferguson*, which held that separate but equal was enough to satisfy the Equal Protection Clause of the Fourteenth Amendment. This validated a nationwide way of life, but particularly the Mississippi way of life. The "separate" part of the ruling was rigidly enforced throughout much of the South, certainly in Mississippi. The "equal" part, however, received only lip service, leading to Negro facilities and opportunities that were inferior in almost all respects.

At the time of the Dixiecrat revolt from the Democratic Party in 1948, provoked by President Harry Truman's modest civil rights proposals, Mississippi Governor Fielding Wright delivered a statewide radio broadcast in which he told African Americans: "If any of you have become so deluded as to want to enter our white schools, patronize our hotels and cafes, enjoy social equality with the whites, then kindness and true sympathy require me to advise you to make your home in some state other than Mississippi." I was just three at the time, so I have no memory of it, but that radio speech illustrates the prevailing attitude of white Mississippi that I would soon hear for myself, most notably from subsequent governors like Ross Barnett and Paul Johnson from 1959 to 1967.

After the *Brown* decision in 1954, Mississippi had quickly become a leading edge of what came to be called "massive resistance" to desegregation. This strategy to defeat, obstruct, and delay was a South-wide phenomenon, but Mississippi contributed two significant components of it. The first was the White Citizens' Councils, which originated in northwest Mississippi within months of *Brown* and by 1956 had hundreds of chapters across the Southern states. The Councils were somewhat of a "white-collar KKK," relying on social pressure and economic reprisals rather than outright violence to keep both blacks and whites from stepping outside the bounds of the Mississippi way of life. The second was the State Sovereignty Commission, created by an act of the legislature in 1956. Gestapo-like, the Commission was charged to "do and perform any and all acts and things deemed necessary and proper to protect the sovereignty of the State of Mississippi, and her sister states, from encroachment thereon by the federal government." Commission agents spied on and kept extensive files on anyone who attended interracial meetings, participated in any kind of civil rights activity, or even wrote a letter to the editor critical of segregation. The publicly funded Commission routinely shared its information with the White Citizens' Councils.

Propaganda regularly reinforced segregation. Consider two examples. While cleaning up my basement in Oakland many years later, I came across a middle school history book called *Our Mississippi*, authored by Pearl Vivian Guyton, published in 1959. This particular copy had been issued to my sister, Sandy. Out of curiosity, I read a few chapters and was shocked to see how we had been indoctrinated. Under a chapter called "The Problems of Reconstruction," the following racial stereotype appeared:

> For their own good, however, the Negroes were restricted in a number of ways by the terms of the Black Code. The legislators realized that the freed Negroes would not work unless they were made to, and that, if they did not work, they would starve. Consequently, a law was passed requiring all Negroes to find work by the second Monday in January, 1866.

"For their own good?" Really? The "made to" part was true, but for an unstated reason, namely that the Black Codes had become a substitute for slavery in the aftermath of the Civil War.

The textbook glorified the Ku Klux Klan:

> It is not, however, in the nature of Southern people to submit long to indignities and injustice. In 1866, a secret organization, the Ku Klux Klan, was founded in Tennessee. It quickly spread throughout the South. The purpose of the Klan was the protection of weak, innocent, and defenseless people, especially the widows and orphans of the Confederate soldiers. Besides this worthy aim, the Klan had another purpose—that of restoring the political power in the South to the educated and responsible white men who formerly had held it.

Protection of widows and orphans? How about lynchings of blacks and bombings of Sunday school children?

The book presented two pictures of Jefferson Davis, the president of the Confederacy, along with portraits of several Confederate generals, but none of Abraham Lincoln or any Union officer, nor did it even mention that President Lincoln had been assassinated, let alone by a Confederate sympathizer.

A second propaganda machine was our statewide newspaper. Unlike today, the *Clarion-Ledger* in those days raged as exceedingly racist and ever antagonistic to the federal government. Published in Jackson, the *Clarion-Ledger* dominated the media in Mississippi. A regular daily editorial called "Mississippi Notebook" ran under the byline of Tom Ethridge. Bark to core, his column seethed with anger against civil rights reform, the Supreme Court, and the Kennedys. His column brainwashed a hundred thousand readers each day. In time, Ethridge would even set his sights on what would become our small progressive group at Mississippi State University.

The *Clarion-Ledger* gave any news of the federal government or civil rights reform a negative spin. The Bible was regularly invoked to justify the Mississippi way of life. The *Clarion-Ledger* owners also controlled the equally virulent afternoon newspaper, the *Jackson Daily News*. When they reported on a demonstration, the papers would usually focus on any violence and blame the demonstrators (though the violence almost always came from white counter-protestors). Yes, there existed a few moderate, courageous newspaper editors elsewhere in Mississippi (like Hazel Brannon Smith at the *Lexington Advertiser* and Hodding Carter at the *Delta Democrat-Times*), but the Jackson papers dominated the state. My afternoon paper route happened to be with an upstart competitor, the *State-Times,* that eventually went out of business.*

The propaganda worked. One reason it worked was that we lived in

---

* The Old Guard also had allies in local television. In 1955, for example, then attorney and civil rights advocate Thurgood Marshall appeared on the *Today* show on NBC. Our second television station, WLBT, an NBC affiliate, simply pulled the plug—with the screen captioned "Cable Difficulty." It did the same thing when a national broadcast reported on a sit-in at the Woolworth's in Jackson—the local broadcast went dark.

a localized, inbred culture. Air travel remained infrequent, confined to refurbished DC-3s from the war. Jet travel was still developing. Very few national corporations had offices in the state. Television arrived about the time of the Korean War but coverage included only local affairs along with syndicated shows like *I Love Lucy*—not the national conversation that we know today. (One shining exception stood out—the legendary Edward R. Murrow on CBS.) At first, the television networks downplayed the civil rights movement, so we got little criticism of our system. Even the national movie industry portrayed blacks (and all other non-whites) as second-class, reinforcing the idea that the races deserved different treatment. The major league ball games we saw on television had almost no black players—indeed, the last team to integrate, the Red Sox, did not do so until as late as 1959. To keep out ideas that might lead to reforms, the state board that oversaw all colleges and universities in our state prohibited any speaker on any campus who was deemed "controversial." Political correctness meant conformity to the Mississippi way of life.

A distinction existed then, though history has understandably forgotten it, between white segregationists and white supremacists. Our mom and dad fell into a category of whites who wanted segregation but rejected white supremacy. This group conceded, if not fully embraced, that all races were God's creatures and that all were equal under the Constitution (and my parents further believed all God's creatures ought to be welcomed at *any* house of God). White segregationists believed that the "separate but equal" doctrine adopted by the United States Supreme Court in 1896 had been right and that the overturning of that rule in 1954 had been wrong. Separate but equal, they held, supplied all the equality required by the Constitution. Separation of the races, they would say, flowed from the very fact that God had given them different colors of skin. Just as it was natural for birds of a feather to flock together, it was natural, they argued, for the different races to keep to themselves. They conceded that all "qualified" citizens, blacks included, should be allowed to vote, yet they approved of the idea of voter qualification tests to prevent "the unqualified" from voting, which, as applied, inevitably resulted in the disenfranchisement of black voters. This group opposed violence. They felt that lynch mobs and those who killed civil rights workers or bombed churches should be prosecuted, but they remained careful, even fearful, in saying so.

By contrast, the white supremacists not only insisted on segregation but also regarded blacks as a subclass—perhaps freed from slavery, but unworthy of equal privileges. White supremacists regretted that the United States Supreme Court had ever gone so far as to embrace "separate but equal," for they rejected the "equal" half of the doctrine. There was no need for equal treatment, they held, for the effort would be wasted. One of several infamously racist Mississippi officials, Theodore Bilbo, remarked that "teaching a nigger to read and write is just ruining a good cotton picker." Mostly in rural areas, white supremacists not only included Klan members but their sympathizers. Many white supremacists approved outright of lynchings, murder, bombings, burnings, and terrorism of all kinds, even the murder of children, claiming to find justification for their hatred and violence in Christianity. Even if a white supremacist didn't approve of a particular murder, he would nevertheless shrug his shoulders and say the victim should have known better than to buck the Mississippi way of life.

Cross burnings were the work of the white supremacists, specifically the Klan. I heard about cross burnings but never actually saw one. Mother saw one, however. In 1963, just before midnight, she was driving home from her nursing shift. Her route wove through downtown Jackson. Where Lynch Street met Terry Road, part of a black residential area, a large cross blazed on the median of the roadway, set afire by racists to terrorize the black population during a frenzied period when all of Jackson remained gripped by civil rights demonstrations. It scared my mother to death. She felt its heat as she drove by. She accelerated, then ran every red light all the way home. I was still up when she arrived and remember even now how she trembled, the fear in her voice. If a burning cross could terrorize a white woman who just happened to be driving by, how much more would it terrorize the black residents of Jackson for whom it was intended?

The vast majority of white Mississippi fell into either the white supremacy group or the white segregationist camp, more in the latter than the former. History has rightly denounced both viewpoints, but, at the time, those like my mom and dad in the segregation camp viewed themselves as decent, law-abiding, even compassionate. My dad employed a crew foreman named Hack, an African American, and trusted him like family. And our parents helped support a black family whose mother, Ivory, had worked for us when Sandy and I were infants in the late 1940s. Even after Ivory moved away, she and her son would still visit. I played with her son, and Mom and Dad gave them clothes and goods, hand-me-downs, even cash. When Ivory died, around 1950, we attended her funeral out in the country. Our entire family went. We wore our Sunday best, the only whites in an old black Mississippi church, completely packed. It became our turn to sit in the rear. Ivory lay in the open casket down front surrounded by a garden of flowers. She had helped introduce us kids to life. Now, she introduced us to death.*

It would not be too much to say that my parents looked down on the white supremacists and felt kindness toward the ordinary black family. They felt no kindness, however, toward those trying to end segregation. The reality was that both segregationists and supremacists kept whites in power and elected politicians who ran against "Kennedy liberals" and integration. Both groups favored preservation of the Mississippi way of life.

Only a sliver of the white demographic in Mississippi rated as progressive. They rejected white supremacy *and* racial segregation. Called "nigger lovers" by hidebound racists, this category believed everyone should have the right to vote, blacks included, and suspected that voter qualification tests were just a gimmick to deny the franchise to blacks. Only within this progressive category could even qualified support be found for equal opportunity in employment or public accommodations. The generally accepted progressive (white) view maintained that employers or cafes or hotels should be free, if they chose, to hire or serve without regard to race. That is, no law or custom should *prohibit* equality of treatment, but it should be a matter of individual conscience for each employer or proprietor to decide, not a decision to be made for us one way in Washington or the other way in Jackson. This sliver of thought resided mainly on the fringes of a few college campuses.

---

* With the exception of the brief period just described, we never had any "help." Nor did almost anyone we knew. We lived on the south side of Jackson, the working class part of town. It was the north side, the wealthy end of town, that regularly had "help." And Ivory used the same bathroom (our house had only one then) as the rest of us.

Today, of course, most Americans (and most Mississippians) believe in a society in which everyone, regardless of race, should enjoy equal opportunity in everything—including voting, education, employment, marriage, public accommodations, public service, and social standing. But except for rare standouts like author Eudora Welty and Professor Jim Silver, the Ole Miss professor who wrote *Mississippi: The Closed Society*, such views remained exceedingly rare among whites in Mississippi in the 1950s and 1960s. (My sister Willanna, I believe, belonged in this rare group.)

As poor as Mississippi remained compared to the rest of America, our black citizens had it worst of all. Forty-two percent of our population was African American and a third or more of them, by my guess, lived in one- or two-room shacks with tarpaper or cardboard walls, heated by wood stoves without municipal water, electricity, or sewer services. One such tarpaper ghetto occupied the flood plain of the Pearl River near Highway 80—no grass yards, no paved roads, just mud, dirt, and ramshackle huts. Perhaps half of all black families had at least some municipal services and lived in small but barely habitable homes, poor but proud. A few (like the family of Medgar Evers, field secretary for the NAACP in Mississippi) lived in modern, all-black subdivisions. Black schoolkids, by law, could attend only black schools. Their moms and dads, for the most part, worked at jobs for whites—domestic help or sanitation workers or laborers. If they "stepped out of line" by registering to vote (or trying to), they would almost certainly lose their jobs, their homes, and possibly their lives. It took immense courage for any African American to challenge the Mississippi way of life.

Slavery still cast a persistent, evil shadow over Mississippi. Just as the advantages of wealth had passed from one generation to the next, the heartache of poverty had passed from one generation to the next. Everyone freed from bondage was guaranteed a place at the front of the poverty line. A hundred years later in Mississippi, their descendants were still struggling with the same burdens. We could see it, if we wanted to, any day we looked.

As 1963 arrived, the Civil Rights Act of 1964, the Voting Rights Act of 1965, and the Fair Housing Act of 1968 seemed like impossibilities, not even within our comprehension. Those laws rightly belong in the pantheon of our core national principles, certainly the most important legislation in my lifetime. But back in 1963, they were not part of America's fabric. The prevailing regime remained firmly anchored in place.

All of our institutions in Mississippi—the media, the churches, the schools, the police, the customs, the law itself—aligned themselves to support and solidify segregation, relentlessly denying civil rights, especially voting rights, to keep things as they were, our own apartheid. In everyday life, it did not seem as grotesque as it really was—the system appeared as an established *modus vivendi* in which both races accepted their lot and worked hard to provide their children with a step up the ladder. Growing up, that was the way life came at us. Ever so perniciously, it became what we knew, and what we knew became natural to accept. We suffered the handicap of being young, as William Faulkner put it. We wanted to believe in something. We believed in our parents, the heroic generation that had survived the Great Depression, then won the war. We wanted to believe in them.

Today, it seems impossible that good citizens would have accepted such a way of life; but they did—we did, at least at first. But our parents also taught us decency and fairness, and, in time, decency and fairness would win out.

4

Separate But Equal All Over Again

It's 2009 and Barack Obama has just taken office. Gay marriage remains an issue that won't go away. Our president, along with most of America, opposes gay marriage and says that gays and lesbians should be satisfied with civil unions, which confer most of the benefits of marriage in the states that authorize them, but carry no federal protections or benefits. The issue won't go away because gays want full equality. Those old enough to remember the fifties and sixties, I think to myself, surely must see that civil unions for gays but marriage for heterosexuals looks like "separate but equal" all over again. Nevertheless, in 2009, many decent people accept this system anyway, including our president—just as fifty years earlier my parents, along with other decent people, accepted "separate but equal" under Jim Crow.

5

Catastrophe

Dad sensed his own end. We all did. His diabetes remained severe, ever debilitating. Despite the pain, he rose early every morning to work. One evening, after we'd returned from the Texas funeral for Pop, he asked me to massage his leg muscles, which were cramping painfully. I did. They felt like hard rubber. We sat alone on the edge of his bed. His eyes glistened. I could tell that he wanted to say something indelible but the words never formed. Finally, I told him I loved him. He absorbed it in pain, in silence. In his last two years, ambulances took him to emergency rooms half a dozen times, almost always for a diabetic seizure. He once went temporarily blind at our dinner table. One of us phoned for an ambulance while he suffered on the floor beside Mother, his emergency nurse, pressing a tablespoon against his tongue as he writhed in delirium. We lived in dread of those crises.

In November 1960, just before the election of John F. Kennedy, they called me to the front office at Provine High School. I feared the worst. Someone rushed Sandy and me to the hospital, where Dad had gone the night before. We saw him, unable to respond, in his death throes. Then he went still, gone.

The funeral became an ordeal for us—and in a curious way, was scarred by the race controversy. Just as we had been welcomed at Ivory's church, our mom and dad, despite their general support of segregation, felt that anyone of any race should be welcomed at any house of God. This had also been the view of the pastor at our little Presbyterian church, but in the controversial aftermath of the school desegregation decision, he was fired in favor of a whites-only preacher. My dad had liked the old pastor and was against the switch, so he stopped attending church. He didn't raise a fuss; he just didn't go. Mother, Sandy, and I continued to attend. We kids were oblivious to the reason for the change. When our dad died, the replacement reverend conducted the funeral service. Commenting on our dad's poor attendance record after the change in pastors, he had the nerve to tell the mourners that he couldn't say whether or not our dad would go to heaven. Mother never got over this. I wouldn't have either, but, at fifteen, the whole death-and-funeral ordeal had me in such a daze that nothing actually registered.

The cause of death turned out to be an intestinal infection from his war years in North Africa, rather than the diabetes the doctor had assumed. The infection had crippled him badly during the war, then flared up again fifteen years later to kill him. During the Persian Gulf War in the nineties, the Army traced this type of infection to sand lice, but its cause was unknown in the sixties. As he'd told us in his war diary, he'd slept in a pup tent on the ground in Algeria.

I took this photo of Dad in Gulfport in 1958, one of few photographs I made in Mississippi

After Dad died, we had few resources to fall back on. Mother became the head of the family. I became the man of the house. All of the male chores, including fixing things, oiling the attic fan, yard work, replacing shingles, feeding the cattle (until they were sold), and so on, fell to me, and I dutifully did them—but at fifteen, my paper route money wasn't going to support the family.

In light of Dad's illness, Mother had returned to the workplace in the last few months of his life. She had been away from her profession for almost twenty years, so it was hard for her to find work. She applied to St. Dominic Hospital in Jackson and offered to work for free until she had proved herself.

Mother agonized over whether we could make ends meet. She briefly considered placing Sandy and me in some kind of church care (a place called French Camp) until Willanna finished college. She worried, too, that we wouldn't be safe while she was at work. Sandy and I insisted we'd be fine and could get by, so Mother continued on with her nursing career. She usually took the three-to-eleven shift so that she could be with us during some of our waking hours and some of our sleeping hours. She eventually became the head obstetrics nurse at the hospital.

Thanks to her—only to her—we made ends meet. Her insistence on an autopsy, moreover, was what revealed Dad's war-related cause of death, which led to VA college benefits for us kids (and, a few years later, to her insisting, with my blessing, that the draft board reclassify me as the sole surviving son of a soldier who had died from a war-related wound or disease). By the time of my high school graduation, Mother regained her confidence in her skills, but that first year after Dad's death took a heavy toll on her. She remained quiet, reserved, unopinionated, uncomplaining, and always self-sacrificing, in the best meaning of those terms. However hard it was on us, it became very much harder on her. She had been so dependent on our dad's breadwinning and financial judgment that the sudden need to provide for her children added many wrinkles to her loving face. His death and the financial blow it dealt drove home to us kids that we had very little to fall back on and reminded us that we ought to study like hell, and work like hell, to get somewhere in life.

6

Pals

As parents sometimes say to their children, "Show me your friends, and I'll show you your future."

I'd just turned five. Exploring, my sister Sandy, then three, and I threaded our way through our tall, steamy, itchy cornfield to its far edge. From there we had looked across a dirt lane to check out a house through its various stages of construction. This time the house seemed completed. Even better, a mom and dad with a young boy were moving boxes from a car to the house. The boy, who was my size, could see us standing at the edge of the cornfield. We saw him glancing over. To him, we must have seemed like natives emerging from the jungle.

We had no training for this kind of social situation, never having met another kid on our own before, but we wound up guessing at the right thing to do. We crossed the dirt lane (eventually Colonial Drive), said hello, explained who we were, then asked who they were and what was going on. This passed for an introduction. The boy replied that he was Hubert Spottswood Feild Jr., a mouthful understandably shortened to Junior. They were moving into their new house, he said. I gave him a handful of corn kernels, an odd gesture. We became instant pals, our days to be filled with classic boyhood pastimes of rural America. Our backyard chicken coop, until our dad later removed it to suburbanize our lot, served as our first hangout. Never mind that it reeked of poultry poop. Junior's yard and our large side field (the cornfield eventually planted in grass) became Grand Central Station for our ever-larger circle of friends to whom our moms served ample Kool-Aid and pimento cheese sandwiches.

Junior liked to issue dares. When we got our first cap pistols in the second grade, we decided to "hold up" the small general store across Terry Road. I am sure it was Junior's idea, a dare. Nell, the proprietor, a gelatinous lady, was helping a customer, her back to me, as I leapt through the open doorway to fire my gun, which had been upgraded with rubber bands on the hammer plus extra caps packed in the chamber for a louder bang. I told them to reach for the sky. Nell seemed to lift off the floor. Her eyes became impressively magnified as she and her gingham dress whirled about, trembling in terror. Junior never fired his gun. In fact, I submit, he never even entered the store. Having scared the bejesus out of Nell, suddenly realizing my pal was absent, I fled to find him behind a magnolia, rolling in convulsive hysterics.

Our dads confiscated the cap guns.

Science fascinated us, and we took on low-budget science projects. For example, we ran our own battery-operated telephone system between our houses with the help of Junior's dad, who worked for the phone company. Thanks also to his dad, and our own ingenuity, we learned about telescopes, shortwave radio, time capsules, and lighter-than-air balloons, the latter of which led to our small contribution to the space program.

The Soviet Union had become the first nation into space with Sputnik in 1957—a milestone that shocked America. Our country seemed slow to catch up. To advance our cause in space, Junior and I launched vehicles into a suborbital flight. It was 1961. We were fifteen. I disconnected our space heater to get at the gas jet on the screen porch so we could fill long plastic laundry bags with lighter-than-air natural gas. I never would have tried this, of course, if my dad had still been alive. (And no reader should try it for manifest reasons of danger.)

Skyward soared our makeshift aircraft with a passenger aboard: a cricket in an old pill container, along with a notice about our science experiment requesting that the finder of the balloon please call 33773, our home number. We wanted to see if a living creature could survive high altitude. Using Junior's military surplus tracking telescope (which had dual scopes for two users), we watched our balloon rise to glisten many thousands of feet above us before drifting out of sight. About two hours after liftoff, our phone rang.

*(Clockwise from above)
Me, Hound Dog, Sandy,
and Junior Feild (c.
1957); me and Junior
as Cub Scouts (1953);
Junior and Hound Dog
during high school; me
and Joe Turnage where
our cornfield once stood
(1962); Ron Goodbread
in high school (1962)*

I answered. The breathless and excited voice of a grown man reported that he had been mowing his yard when a shiny craft flew down the street. He chased it until it crashed and retrieved the capsule. (Thank God he wasn't smoking.) "Was the occupant alive?" I asked. "Yes. It was alive," he replied earnestly, as if testifying before NASA. Great. Mission accomplished. Check off that box. Crickets could survive high altitude.

ONE OF THE NEIGHBORHOOD kids who saw through the Mississippi way of life sooner than most was Joe Turnage. Our friendship had its roots in science, not politics. Junior and I went in with Joe to build a plywood robot for a grade school science project. It amounted only to a mock-up but looked good, about three feet tall, moving with the help of roller skates and a small electric motor. Its eyes lit up. Otherwise, it could perform no real robot tricks. Nonetheless, a picture of our creation made it into the newspaper, so we beamed with pride.

Joe lived in a prewar subdivision a little closer to town than we did, just off the other side of Terry Road, not far from that rumored Civil War hospital. He had a knack for science and math, an aptitude that would eventually earn him a doctorate in nuclear engineering from MIT. One Christmas I got a chemistry set, so we joined up for a series of experiments. We made both visible and invisible inks, among other things. In our large side yard, where we launched our balloons, we marveled at the night sky, convincing ourselves that intelligent life thrived out there, all but praying for a UFO.

As we reached our teenage years, Joe became the suave member of our little group. He read *Playboy*, which he bragged was contraband in Mississippi. He devoured novels, even poems. A hip poem called "Dog" by Lawrence Ferlinghetti from a hip book called *A Coney Island of the Mind* fell from Joe's lips. So cool. He wore cashmere. With a medium build, Joe had blue eyes and blue-gray glasses. He wore his limp blonde hair long enough to part. He enjoyed arranging it just so, primping. Joe personified class. He loved it. Cheapness offended him. Once at a soda fountain, as we paid our bill near the exit, he frowned at a rack of rank tabloids, then asked the clerk how much they were. Ten cents each, she said. He grabbed the lot of them, tossed them in the trash by the register, smacked a silver dollar on the counter, said "keep the change," then cruised out the door.

Despite his suave affect, Joe was still a bit nerdy, like me. And, like most of us, he stood in awe of young women, goddesses. Joe was Richard Dreyfus in *American Graffiti*, yearning to be Hugh Hefner in *Playboy*.

An amateur magician, Joe dazzled us with sleight of hand and card tricks, but gambling became his main thing. His two favorite phrases were "deal 'em" and "gamble, gamble, gamble." He had stupefying luck at cards. Once, out of the blue, I challenged him to tell me the card on the top of a deck I had shuffled over and again—he got it right in one try!

Joe and I attended the same all-white church. In Sunday school, we had a song that went "Red and yellow, black and white, they are precious in His sight . . . Jesus loves the little children of the world" to underscore the universality of Christianity. But we had only whites in our church, so this did not add up. The logo on the church bulletin said, "Come unto me all who are weary and heavy laden and I shall give you rest," quoting Jesus. As teenagers, about the time the civil rights movement gathered steam, Joe and I would sarcastically pencil "White Only" onto the bulletins and plant them in the hymnals for someone to find later.

One more thing—Joe's mom would save our asses in high school.

RON GOODBREAD, INSTIGATOR OF the billboard affair, became another friend who questioned the Mississippi way of life, as close to a dissident as we had—a cranky one at that. We met in the fifth grade.

Ron's family moved around a lot in the Deep South, mainly due to his dad's need to find work as a carpenter. His dad liked to say that he came into this world with nothing and still had most of it left. His mother could barely read and write. When Ron's parents couldn't afford to raise him, his Aunt Bee, his dad's sister, a sassy divorcée with no kids, took him in to provide the basic necessities—which for Ron meant Coca-Colas, cinnamon rolls, and, most of all, Superman comics. Ron insisted on giving us Kryptonian names like Joe-El and Bill-El, reserving Zor-Ron for himself.

Even before high school, Ron could write well and type professionally, his aunt being a crack typist and secretary. He invariably wore a white dress shirt, black pants, and black shoes. No blue jeans. No madras shirts. Always black pants with a long-sleeved white shirt. He stood tall, skinny, and with black horn-rimmed glasses, his face often wore a quizzical look—except when he was charming a young woman or holding forth on politics or history. He was sarcastic, funny, and a hypochondriac.

While my dad was alive, he referred to Ron derisively as "Long Hair." Ron's Elvis-style hair was longer than most (but not nearly as long as hippies would wear in a few years). In truth, Dad never warmed to Ron's nonconformist ways or crappy diet. Once, Ron stayed overnight. At our family breakfast the next morning he received bacon, eggs, grits, biscuits, and milk. Unimpressed, Ron merely rearranged every item on his plate to create the illusion that he was eating, but there was no fooling my dad, who sat there in stony silence until he erupted with an order for Long Hair to eat everything on his plate. Ron could bring himself to swallow only a fraction of it. Meanwhile, every other plate at the table was clean. Painful. Finally, my dad left in a storm of maxims and profanity.

Mother, on the other hand, adored Ron and treated him as another son, especially after Dad died. No maxims from her. Nor profanity. To boot, Ron had a platonic but relentless crush on Willanna, who had turned into a curvaceous Natalie Wood look-alike. In fact, Ron was constantly attracted to women and became superb at charming them. He eventually enjoyed a successful career of consecutive marriages.

Ron didn't share our love for science. He tried his best to dissuade me, Joe, and Junior from doing science projects or entering science fairs, calling them "just a bunch of worry-burry." Nor did he excel at cards, dice, or gambling. Unlike Joe, when it came to games of chance, Ron was a fugitive from the law of averages, to borrow a phrase from Bill Mauldin. With dice, he invariably would throw snake eyes just when it would hurt him most.

History, not science or chance, consumed Ron. By high school, he had become a voracious reader of history. His hero, Abraham Lincoln, gave him a Republican bent. After mastering all six volumes of the Carl Sandburg work on Lincoln, Ron recounted for us, step-by-step, the assassination and its aftermath. He recited the Gettysburg Address and Lincoln's second inaugural address from memory. Ron understood who had won the Civil

War, a question seemingly still in play in those days. He saw the Old Guard doctrine of states' rights as a cousin of the old attitude that had brought on the rebellion. Ron had only contempt for those Mississippi politicians who defied federal authority. For Ron, federal authority meant President Lincoln and his successors. We had to respect it, he thought. As a close pal then, some of his attitudes made sense to me, particularly the supreme role of federal authority. Somebody had to be the boss, I gathered. Logic pointed to the central government. In those days, the concept of federalism and the supreme role of federal authority was rejected in Mississippi, but we were fortunate to get the straight scoop from Ron.

In high school, Ron refused to take part in the daily pledge of allegiance. In Jackson, the pledge had been a schoolhouse ritual since at least the Second World War, if not 1896 when it was adopted by Congress. Ron thought that the daily mumbling by students had made a mockery of the sacred pledge, rendering it almost meaningless. He said that his loyalty to his country was not so fragile that it had to be renewed every day. As all other students stood to face the flag each morning, Ron sat at his desk in respectful silence. His refusal became well-known in the school. Still, Ron was liked school-wide, with one major exception—the principal. Like my dad, Principal Hal France disliked Ron. He looked for an excuse to expel him. Principal France, however, knew enough to know that even in Mississippi you couldn't expel a student for refusing to pledge allegiance. He kept his powder dry, waiting.

7

The Right of Protest

In April 1962, Principal France finally thought he had his chance to expel Ron—and his pals.

It all involved our club, the Higgen Hogs, also known as "the HH." It had originated years earlier as a playground team in grade school. In high school, we reconvened for a more serious purpose but kept the name. Yes, the name was ridiculous, but the organization was not. Ron, Joe, Junior, and I were members; there were about a dozen of us altogether, almost all excellent students, including three National Merit finalists. We adopted a constitution. Its preamble proclaimed that the organization had been "established for the purpose of learning the value of order, respect for good government, to further the advancement of honest activities in which we can participate and the endorsement of a free society," all Ron's wordsmithing. We held regular meetings, discussed current events, fielded a sandlot baseball team, organized a cheering section at school football games, went camping, and, most of all, gave each other moral support. At school, the Higgen Hogs had a reputation as decent, considerate, even slightly progressive. Most of the teachers liked us.

Nevertheless, we got in trouble—big trouble. After the senior class presidency for the coming year was won by one of our HH members, Bennett Price, Principal France canceled the election and declared the runner-up the winner. The alleged reason was that the winner's grades fell a tiny fraction below the required level for senior class president. Not fair, we thought. We wondered why this defect had not disqualified him *before* the election since his grades had been fully known then as well. Why was this concern only being raised *after* the vote? Was it because the principal's favorite had come in second?

Ron and I decided to circulate a protest in the form of a mimeographed sheet called "The Higgen-Hog Hacker." This name was ridiculous too, but it had a plausible purpose ("to hack" meant to gripe). Our sheet laid out our grievance, asking why the grade issue had surfaced only after the fact, a form of election rigging. We cut a stencil on the old Royal typewriter at my house, then used a hand-cranked mimeograph machine to run off thirty-five copies.

The next morning in front of the school, we stood ready to hand them out, but Ron and I started to get cold feet. Calling us "chickenshits," our HH comrade Carl Dicks snatched them from our hands and passed them out. Those thirty-five copies spread like wildfire. Within an hour, virtually all nine hundred students in all grades had read one. The vast majority of students and teachers, we would come to realize, agreed with us.

That morning, we waited for the ax to fall. We didn't have to wait long. In second period, I was playing left field in physical education class when Coach Howard Shook motioned me in and told me to report to the principal's office. I was in deep shit and knew why. The coach showed a hint of a smile in his eyes, his way of suggesting that he knew what we had done and wished us well. It took some time for all of the Hogs to assemble in the principal's office. When I arrived, Ron already sat there composing himself for the barrage to come. Carl sat there, too, calmest of all, rather hoping, I suspected, that we'd all get "canned," another of his favorite words. I took a seat, imagining how bad it would get and how I would explain this to my mom.

When all twelve or so of us had jammed into the room, Principal France waved a copy of the newsletter about, calling it "crap" and an "insult" to him and his administration. He then said that we were a bunch of no-account kids involved in some kind of "subversive organization," illegal, he said, under state law. Carl gazed at Principal France with his "you are so full of shit" smile but said nothing. Ron and I spoke up and said that we had prepared the broadside on our own, that all the others were blameless.

*Bennet Price, Ron Goodbread, Joe Turnage, and me at the Vicksburg
Battlefield (1963)*

Principal France replied that people like us were "going to wind up some
day in Leavenworth Penitentiary."

Warming to the occasion, France said that he understood that one of
us would not even pledge allegiance to the flag, pretending not to know
who it was.

Ron raised his hand and said, "That would be me."

Principal France excoriated Ron, demanding to know why he would
not stand and say the pledge. Ron explained that the uninspired way we
performed the ritual made a mockery of the flag.

Agitated and angry, Principal France retorted, curiously injecting the
issue of the Civil War, "Listen, son, I will pledge allegiance to the flag of
the United States, to the flag of the State of Mississippi, and to the flag of
the Confederate States of America."

In response to this last item—the rebel flag—Ron firmly replied, his
hero Abe Lincoln in mind, "Mr. France, you can't pledge allegiance to the
flag of the United States *and* to the flag of the rebellion that tried to destroy
it—that would be treason."

Jesus Christ and General Jackson, we all thought, Ron, you've done it now.

Upon hearing the word treason, Principal France soared from angry to apoplectic. Every blood vessel in his neck, face, and head bulged; his eyes dilated; his brows splayed. He gesticulated, sputtered. Verging on incoherence, even meltdown, he waved his arms, then managed to pronounce a group sentence: All of us would be suspended—subject only to his meeting first with our parents.

"Get the hell out, leave," he ordered.

Ron and I felt terrible for having gotten our pals in so much trouble without having put it to a vote first. We should never have presumed to speak for all the others. Still, no one took the easy way out. Everyone took the heat. Returning to our classrooms, for once we, not the jocks, got standing ovations.

The threat of suspension, however, lasted only one day. Here's where Joe's mom saved us. Those parents who could came the next day. To his surprise, the principal got an earful, especially from Mrs. Ollion Turnage, Joe's mom. A frontier woman who spent much of her life in Arizona, she could be fierce. As the senior parent present, she tore into Principal France, telling him what a tinhorn he was. There he was, she said, proposing to suspend the top students in the class for doing nothing more than exercising their right of peaceful protest against his interference with the school election. What kind of principal, she demanded, would do such a misguided thing? What happened to the First Amendment? What kind of principal would set aside a school election and declare a new winner based on a supposed problem he had realized all along? Yes, she said. She knew all about these kids and their club—she had even hosted a big Mexican dinner for them— they were the best. Mrs. Turnage proved more than Principal France could handle. He reversed himself—or got reversed—and we stayed in school, thanks to Joe's mom and the First Amendment.

8

Blowing in the Wind

In 1957, Little Rock, Arkansas, became the first battleground over desegregation in the South after the *Brown* decision. On September 2 of that year, Governor Orval Faubus sent the Arkansas National Guard to all-white Central High School, not to control the hostile white mob assembled outside but to prevent nine black students, known as the Little Rock Nine, from registering for classes and integrating the school. Several weeks later, a federal district judge ordered the governor to remove the National Guard, and the Little Rock Nine were able to enter Central High School under Little Rock police escort. However, riots broke out, and, unable to control the mob, the police rushed the black students out of the school. The next day, President Eisenhower federalized the Arkansas National Guard and sent paratroopers from the 101st Airborne Division to Little Rock to escort the Little Rock Nine back into the school. The soldiers remained for the entire school year, guarding the black students.

I was twelve. It was about the same time the shanty schoolhouse in the sand quarry made an impression on me. The grainy black-and-white images arrived on our small television—troops with black school kids entering Central High amidst a jeering white crowd. President Eisenhower gave a televised speech to the nation. He said the law of the land must be obeyed. The use of Army troops, the same army that had fought the Germans, to safeguard school children had no precedent. So it was big news. I thought about the fear inside those kids, intensified by the cruelty of the hostile crowd. Why would those kids do this to themselves? I asked. What did they have against their own school? Would this happen at our school?

The news out of Arkansas and the specter of school desegregation swept race-baiting officials into office in Mississippi, most notably Governor Ross Barnett in 1959, then Paul Johnson, his successor, in 1963, both of whom pledged to stand against the federal government to resist all integration. Barnett once said that "God made niggers black because they are so mean and evil." Barnett and Johnson were backed by the White Citizens' Council, the State Sovereignty Commission, the Ku Klux Klan, and the vast majority of registered voters in our state.

Soon after the election of Ross Barnett, the Freedom Riders put Jackson on the front pages of the nation's press with the first highly publicized event of the civil rights movement in Mississippi. The Freedom Riders—African Americans and white activists—rode the interstate buses to protest the continued segregation of public transportation throughout the South. In Washington, D.C., on May 4, 1961, the Freedom Riders boarded two buses bound for New Orleans. On May 24, 1961, when I was fifteen, the Freedom Riders reached the Trailways bus depot in Jackson.

It made the evening national news, then a short broadcast of only a quarter-hour. It was the first time I saw anything on national television that I had seen for myself, namely, our local bus station. Our grandfather from Texas, Pop, had arrived and left from it each summer in the 1950s. Ironically, the bus depot and train station had become the only places in all of Jackson where the separate facilities had actually lived up to the equal part—black and white waiting rooms, restrooms, and food counters were similar. Federal regulations eventually required integration of rail and bus terminals, but, in violation of federal law, local law continued to uphold the segregated facilities. The *Clarion-Ledger* harped that the dual facilities were equal (again, for once, this was mostly true) and that the only people complaining were outsiders. Upon their arrival in Jackson, the Freedom Riders were promptly arrested and jailed. As more and more Freedom Riders arrived, the jails filled up and many of the Riders were housed at Parchman Farm, the notorious Mississippi State Penitentiary.

I wondered about this. In Little Rock, peaceful black kids had been escorted by soldiers to school. In Jackson, peaceful black bus riders were taken by police to jail. What exactly accounted for the difference? Our local officials kept saying that the communists were behind desegregation. Why, then, had the president sent in troops to protect the students in Little Rock? These were pieces of a puzzle I hadn't yet fitted together. My diary's pithy entries concentrated on girls, school, church, a project to build a pinball machine, chemistry-set experiments, time capsules, dirt-clod wars, and our neighborhood olympics. I was fascinated by organized crime and law enforcement, especially Eliot Ness and his Untouchables. I had no coherent view of the race crisis unfolding around us.

9

Camelot and Cuba

As President Eisenhower's last term wound down, we realized that he'd been the only chief executive our generation of baby boomers had really known. For us, therefore, the presidential election in 1960 became a phenomenon. On the Republican side, the vice president, Richard Nixon, sought to capitalize on the popularity of Ike and his famous smile. Mother favored Nixon. On the Democratic side, Senator John F. Kennedy of Massachusetts emerged as the front runner in the primaries. During the summer of 1960, Senator Lyndon Johnson of Texas challenged Kennedy for the nomination. The South, which was solidly Democratic, supported Johnson. Dad favored Johnson. Both were Texans. Mom and Dad argued over their favorite candidates.

The Johnson boomlet, however, proved too little too late. Kennedy won the nomination in July, despite the fact that we'd never before had a Catholic president. Kennedy blunted this issue with a convincing speech in Houston, putting to rest most fears that he would take orders from the Vatican. Nixon thought he could whip JFK in a debate. They agreed to go at it in our nation's first televised presidential debate. It became a turning point in the election. On the screen, Kennedy looked tanned and confident whereas Nixon looked like he had been worked over by a mortician. (Radio listeners, however, thought Nixon got the better of Kennedy in the debate.) Kennedy won the general election, just barely. The Kennedy-Johnson ticket carried six southern states—but not Mississippi, which went for Senator Harry F. Byrd of Virginia. My dad did not live to cast his vote. He died six days before the general election.

Our new president gleamed with glory—he was a war hero, attractive, witty, smart, a student of history, even a Pulitzer Prize-winning author. Our new First Lady sparkled with beauty and class. The president's brother, Robert, our new attorney general, came across as energetic and fierce. They weren't fat or stodgy like most politicians. They all had style. After the assassination of the president in November 1963, the term Camelot was used to describe those thousand days of Kennedy charisma. The term captured perfectly the charm that the Kennedys had brought to Washington. Even in the South, the Kennedys' signature class and grace became reasons to like the new First Family.

APART FROM CHARM, ANOTHER reason to support the Kennedys was our need to stand with the president to contain communism, which was then spreading around the globe at an alarming rate—including right under our noses in Cuba.

Cuba dominated the headlines. In 1959, after waging a successful revolution against President Fulgencio Batista, Fidel Castro became prime minister of Cuba and was recognized by the United States, until Castro's communism was soon revealed. Holy Cow! Now, we had a blood enemy just ninety miles off our shore. Early in the Kennedy Administration came the Bay of Pigs debacle, a CIA-inspired invasion to oust Castro from power. It failed at the water's edge. JFK took complete responsibility (even though the invasion plan had been cooked up during the Eisenhower Administration), an act of statesmanship amidst the ruin of failure that ironically caused Kennedy's public support to skyrocket.

Then, in October 1962, came the Cuban missile crisis. The CIA discovered Soviet medium-range ballistic missiles in Cuba, capable of hitting Washington, D.C. Behind closed doors in the White House, military and national security advisors, we now know, urged air strikes against all missile sites in Cuba. The president worried, however, that such air strikes could lead to a retaliatory nuclear strike against the United States or to a Soviet attack on West Berlin, another Cold War hot spot. In the latter case, we were so outnumbered that our only effective response would have been tactical nuclear weapons, which then would have led to "all-out thermonuclear war," a phrase much in vogue. All of this was debated in secret at the White House over several days until finally President Kennedy went on the air to alert the nation to the threat so close to home and to tell us that our Navy would throw a quarantine around Cuba to prevent more Soviet ships with missiles from passing through. He demanded the removal of the missiles already in Cuba. He didn't order air strikes, but he didn't take that option off the table.

We were stunned by the president's news—Soviet missiles in Cuba!

But the president had a plan—a Navy quarantine. God, would this work, we wondered? We hovered one heartbeat from a conventional conflict and two heartbeats from an atomic war. It was all we could think about.

The specter of nuclear destruction persisted as the terrifying backdrop for everyday life. We'd all seen the fresh images of the islands of the Bikini Atoll being swallowed by a mushroom cloud and knew, of course, about Hiroshima and Nagasaki. America lagged in the space race. Soviet Premier Nikita Khrushchev boasted that the Soviet Union would "bury" the United States. Communism had already taken over Eastern Europe, China, North Vietnam, and North Korea. The Berlin Wall went up in 1961, during our junior year in high school. In June 1963, as we would be graduating, JFK would stand before the wall to deliver his famous "Ich bin ein Berliner" speech, the single best speech of the Cold War.

America's twin defense policies were "containment" and "mutual assured destruction." As Robert Oppenheimer put it, we were like "two scorpions in a bottle." Terms like ICBM, NORAD, SAC, "missile gap," and strontium-90 punctuated conversation and news reports. The world remained locked in a death struggle: Communism versus Democracy. America believed it. In Jackson, we believed it, black and white alike.

President Kennedy had even called on Americans to install bomb shelters (one of Willanna's friends had one in her backyard). To this end, even before the Cuban missile crisis, one outlet in Jackson began selling oversized septic tank-like containers as underground bomb shelters for backyards in the same way outlets today sell recreational vehicles, placing them in long aboveground rows in a large lot for easy viewing. We got inside one to see what it was like.

"Like rats in a beer can," Carl Dicks observed.

So on that day in October 1962, when President Kennedy went on television to announce the startling news that the Soviet Union had missiles in Cuba capable of reaching much of the United States, those of us in Jackson felt that the doomsday clock had run out of time. My diary entry for October 23 blared in block letters, "EYES ON CUBA." Then, in my usual scrawl, "In international crisis U.S. blockades entry of arms into Cuba. Russian steamers head toward Cuba regardless." My diary entry for October 24 said in big headline letters, "MANY FEAR WWIII," adding, "Russian ships to tangle tomorrow." In Jackson, we figured the enemy would not waste a missile on our little hometown. But we also thought a missile intended for a military base in or near Mississippi might go astray to hit us anyway. Failing that, if a war ensued, lethal radiation clouds would get us, as in the popular post-apocalyptic novel and film *On the Beach*, about the aftermath of a nuclear war. While all of that loomed as the sober downside, as teenagers in the middle of high school we mostly saw the upside, namely the trembling excitement of a vast stage performance.

In the carpool going to school, we fixated on the news coming through the cloth-covered, chrome-ribbed central dashboard speaker. At school, we hung by transistor radios, listening for word on whether the Soviet ships, known to be close to the quarantine line, had yet been challenged. Teachers drilled us in how to shelter in place.

Then, surprisingly, we heard that the Soviet vessels had stopped, dead in the water. What did this mean? We speculated. Maybe a clever ruse. This lasted hours. Tension gripped us. Then the Soviet ships turned around to head away from Cuba. Our hopes brightened. They blossomed when it was announced that the Soviets had agreed to remove the missiles in exchange for our pledge not to invade Cuba and, though this part became public only years later, our further pledge to promptly remove our missiles from Turkey. A major stand-down ensued.

We'd won!

That massive eyeball-to-eyeball showdown—the Soviet fleet versus the American fleet on a collision course, both superpowers bristling with armed nuclear missiles—proved to be as close as our generation has come to all-out atomic war. While the confrontation ended without war, thanks to the prudence of President Kennedy (and Premier Khrushchev), we still took it for granted that there was about a one-in-three chance that our generation would eventually see a nuclear holocaust, the last thunderclap of doom.

With the perspective of years, I believe that the Cuban missile crisis was the single greatest exercise in presidential judgment witnessed in our time. The president's rejection of air strikes in favor of a quarantine (coupled with parallel diplomacy) took courage and wisdom and very likely saved at least fifty million lives in America and the Soviet Union. The Bay of Pigs debacle had served as a caution to the president, a caution to subject the recommendation of his advisors and generals to his own critical analysis. Not all presidents are called upon to make decisions of this magnitude, but some are—so we should never forget that presidential judgment matters.

The Cuban missile crisis also illustrated a paradox. When it came to fighting communism, President Kennedy had no stronger ally than Mississippi and the Deep South. Yet, when it came to fighting racism, he had no stronger enemy, as we shall now see.

10

James Meredith at Ole Miss

The first attempt at school desegregation in Mississippi came in Oxford at the University of Mississippi. Known as Ole Miss and set in planter country not far from Memphis, the university was Mississippi's elite institution of higher education. It was famous as the college that rolled out a Confederate flag the size of the football field at halftime, the rebel yell echoing through the stadium.

In 1961, James Meredith, a twenty-nine-year-old Mississippian and Air Force veteran, applied to transfer from all-black Jackson State College to all-white Ole Miss. Though Meredith was exceedingly qualified, he was rejected, resulting in a sensational confrontation at the outset of the 1962–63 school year, our senior year in high school. The Meredith incident provoked my first diary entries on the subject of civil rights. That was September 1962, just three weeks before the Cuban missile crisis. That year, Ole Miss went undefeated in football, but in the courtroom it suffered a seismic reversal. I was seventeen.

With legal assistance from the NAACP Legal Defense and Education Fund, then directed by Thurgood Marshall, Meredith sued in the United States District Court for the Southern District of Mississippi, asserting that Ole Miss, which had never accepted a black student, had rejected him only on the basis of race. The district court judge ruled against Meredith. But the U.S. Fifth Circuit Court of Appeals in New Orleans reversed the district court's decision and ordered Meredith's admission in June 1962. That brought the story to page one. Ole Miss again blocked Meredith's admission by obtaining (from another appeals court judge) several stays.

Finally, in September 1962, the Supreme Court upheld the Fifth Circuit's original mandate that Meredith be admitted.

Governor Ross Barnett, the son of a Confederate veteran, had been elected in 1959 on a pledge to block every attempt at racial integration. Invoking an antebellum doctrine called "interposition," a states' rights theory, Barnett, along with an angry mob, physically blocked Meredith, who was escorted by federal marshals, from registering. Though the Fifth Circuit court issued a restraining order against Barnett and, a few days later, cited him for contempt, the governor and lieutenant governor continued to deny Meredith's admission. Finally, a convoy of federal marshals escorted Meredith to the Oxford campus on the evening of September 30, 1962. The next day he registered for classes. That is the short version. The longer version is impossible to forget.

On September 20, we sat in the crowded Provine High School cafeteria in Jackson when the most rabid of our classmates leapt atop a formica-top table to announce that the court of appeals had just ordered the Meredith enrollment to go forward. Livid, our classmate said that he would drive up to Oxford to "take care of" Meredith if we would pitch in to pay for the cost of his trip. He glowed with hatred. Thankfully, no one contributed, and no one rose to support him. He was, in fact, ignored, so he left the room in disgust.

At that point, Provine High School itself was still all-white but the reaction in the cafeteria that day said something about the attitudes of the era. The vast majority of students stood ready to accept events as they unfolded, one way or the other, whether they liked it or not (and most did not), but they refused to aid and abet violence. For every hothead who would have reached for a gun, there might have been ninety-nine who would have refused to do so. On the other hand, there *were* hotheads. And one out of a hundred was a significant number of hotheads across the entire state. The (now deceased) guy who stood on the tabletop was a vivid illustration.

Meanwhile, the Jackson papers (both owned by the same right-wing family) fanned the flames, running one item after another exhorting resistance. The *Jackson Daily News* urged readers to form a wall of human flesh around the governor's mansion to prevent service of contempt orders. The

Clarion-Ledger, the morning paper, carried a provocative headline about a "gun battle" shaping up at the university, then reported that retired Army General Edwin Walker, a hero in the Second World War but now a right-wing provocateur, was on his way to Oxford to oppose the enrollment. On the night of Saturday, September 29, a huge crowd gathered at an Ole Miss football game in Jackson where at halftime, Governor Barnett gave an impassioned speech calling for white Mississippians to defend themselves against federal interference. It electrified the crowd and those listening by radio. Hundreds of protesters converged on Oxford.

On Sunday, September 30, when Meredith arrived on campus guarded by federal marshals, the white protest turned into a violent riot. It began with a swelling crowd of thousands around the Lyceum, the main administration building—chants at first, then rocks and bottles and bricks hurled at federal marshals, who responded with tear gas. Though Barnett had promised the Kennedy administration that state patrolmen would help keep order, they were abruptly withdrawn. Suddenly left to fend for themselves, the marshals quickly lost control. The violence escalated during the night, egged on by General Walker, by then on site. The campus reeked of smoke and tear gas. Rioters killed two men, a French journalist and a local white jukebox repairman. Hundreds were wounded. Though President Kennedy had hoped to avoid the use of federal soldiers, he had to send in a force numbering in the thousands to quell the riot.

James Meredith remained under federal guard in his newly assigned dorm room as the chaos unfolded. John Doar and Nicholas Katzenbach of the Justice Department huddled in the Lyceum, directing the federal defense. The riot at Ole Miss became the most violent domestic resistance to federal authority since the Civil War. The next day, October 1, James Meredith enrolled, then attended his first class, guarded by marshals—a historic first.

State officials and others in Mississippi quickly blamed the Kennedy Administration and the federal marshals for precipitating the riot, but there is no doubt that violent racists, encouraged by our governor, the Jackson newspapers, and General Walker, were responsible.

A year later, Bob Dylan immortalized the disgrace in a song called *Oxford Town*.

We now know the truth of what happened, but, as the crisis was unfolding, the Jackson media and the rumor mill were our only sources of information. In that tense ten-day period between Meredith's first attempt to register, which was personally blocked by Barnett, and his eventual admission, I made five diary entries. All five are set out in full here, for they supply a baseline of my attitudes at (barely) seventeen. On Monday, September 24, 1962, I wrote:

> Negro James Mer[edi]th with attorneys with pocketful of court orders was rejected from entering Ole Miss the other day. He will try again tomorrow. Mississippians back Ross. There's going to be trouble, I fear. Showdown at last.

The next entry for Tuesday, September 25, included a reference to the governor's interposition theory:

> Today, around 4:30 p.m., the Hon. Ross R. Barnett of the sovereign state of Mississippi interposed himself, assuming power under his inaugrual [sic] oath and the 10th Amendment of the U.S. Constitution, between Mered[i]th and Federal power and the Ole Miss Registrar.

We now know that "interposition" was a legal theory resurrected by segregationist lawyers from the 1830s "nullification" jurisprudence of South Carolina's John C. Calhoun, which eventually led to secession. The Jackson newspapers, however, presented it to us as accepted bedrock constitutional principle. On Wednesday, September 26, I wrote:

> The State of Mississippi is in Big Trouble. I am anxious for the outcome yet I want it to be unobjectionable. Something's going to give. Mississippi has about 1000 men with support from General Walker and Alabama for more against Marshalls [sic] and troops.

Former General Edwin Walker then enjoyed immense popularity among Southern whites but has since been consigned to "history's ashcan," as famed

conservative William Buckley had the courage to say. Walker had already
retired, so he in no way represented the views of the United States, but that
subtlety was lost on many of us, who, taken in by the propaganda published
in the *Clarion-Ledger*, thought that at least one high-ranking federal officer
supported the governor.

The next day, I wrote:

> Ross Barnett is going to be in trouble. He won't accept any summons
> nor will Lt. Gov. Paul Johnson. They are constantly guarded by state troop-
> ers and no Fed will ever touch them. At any rate, they better not draft me!

The summons were federal court orders to cease and desist from interfer-
ing with the enrollment of James Meredith. On Tuesday, October 2, I wrote:

> Ole Miss, I fear, will soon be rid of one student James Meridith [sic].
> He will soon be killed is the general opinion. Outwardly, I want this to
> happen yet I know it is wrong, so I will try to hope otherwise. The truth
> shall make you free.

These entries reveal an ordinary white kid identifying with his home
state while appreciating the supremacy of federal court orders—a kid who
expected killings would occur but tried to hope otherwise. It is safe to say
that this set of entries, my first on the subject of civil rights, was more South
than North, much influenced by popular attitudes at school, propaganda in
the *Clarion-Ledger*, and political correctness in a closed society.

The riot and killings at Ole Miss upset Ron more than any of us. He
was unmerciful in ridiculing Barnett and his interposition theory. Ron insisted that in any conflict between the national government and the states,
a decision of the national government had to be supreme. Appomattox,
he reminded us, had decided that issue once and for all. So, he concluded
with airtight logic, if federal authority decreed integration, then it had to
be respected. We were close, so my own views were gradually influenced
by Ron. (In five more months, we'd be counter-protesting the "Impeach
Earl Warren" sign.)

Ron's views put him in a distinct minority among whites in Mississippi, even among younger whites. Most students and their parents favored the status quo and resented federal interference. Next door in Alabama, in January 1963, Governor George Wallace proclaimed, "I say segregation now, segregation tomorrow, segregation forever." That was the pervasive majority view.

Worse, Klansmen and demons like our classmate who shouted from the tabletop saw themselves as freedom fighters resisting tyranny in the same way that the underground resisted communism in Eastern Europe. The *Clarion-Ledger* reinforced this view.

11

Utterly Empty

It's 1999. I'm fifty-four. My teenage son, John, and I visit Jackson to explore the remnants of my childhood. Our house at 2325 Terry Road is gone, the large lot scraped off, including Andy's Tree, all replaced by an industrial tire facility. Across the back way, Junior's house remains, though it's vacant now and in extremis after having been converted first to a dentist's office and more recently to a church annex. We walk through his yard. "This pecan tree," I say, gathering a handful of pecans near the tattered house, "is still producing. Can you believe it?" In the old breezeway, I help John imagine Mrs. Feild serving a plate of pimento cheese sandwiches to teenagers circled around a Monopoly game.

We visit Provine High School, all-white in my day but now all-black (the vast majority of whites have abandoned Jackson and its public schools); otherwise, it looks the same. We search the walls in vain for the photograph of our 1960 statewide championship team—all those old photos, we are told, are now archived.

We drive downtown, still less than ten minutes away. At noon, we cruise up Capitol Street, the main thoroughfare, the scene of the boycotts and demonstrations in 1963. Just after we pass the Governor's Mansion, I say, "John, right here on these two corners in those boarded-up buildings were two huge department stores. Back then, at this time on a Saturday, these sidewalks and roads overflowed with people, half white, half black. Totally jammed." John receives all of my commentary in polite silence.

The sidewalks are now empty. No department store remains. Downtown commerce has fled to distant suburbs. In my rear view mirror, I see ten blocks back to the train station. Ahead I see four blocks to the Old Capitol. Amazingly, ours is the only car in *either* direction. Saturday at noon on Capitol Street. Dead as a doornail. Yet I still feel the vibrancy of those Saturday mornings on Capitol Street, that memory more real than the scene before us.

12

Cool Like the Kennedys

Not long after the Cuban missile crisis, President Kennedy's popularity soared again. Adding to the buzz was the "fifty-mile hike," an element of the president's physical fitness initiatives designed to combat the "soft American." The White House had discovered a Teddy Roosevelt executive order challenging Marine officers to walk fifty miles in twenty hours. JFK asked Marine General David M. Shoup to challenge his own Marines to match that feat. He joked that perhaps the White House staff should give it a try—his overweight press secretary, Pierre Salinger, let it be known that he expected an exemption. Attorney General Robert Kennedy actually accomplished the hike—in eighteen hours, through snow and slush and wearing leather oxfords—most impressive!

Then followed a brief nationwide craze of people heeding JFK's call and attempting to match RFK's fifty-mile feat. In Mississippi, some of us wondered whether we could do it.

On Saturday, March 2, 1963, about three weeks after the billboard caper, Ron Goodbread, Carl Dicks, and I set out on our own fifty-mile march to be cool like the Kennedys. This would serve too as our answer to the Provine jocks, who won all the smiles from the young women at school. Possibly even Ann (who reminded us of Jackie Kennedy) would notice. The only wrinkle—none of us had ever hiked more than ten miles before. Our plan was to ramble twenty-five miles along the frontage road by the new interstate highway from Jackson to Crystal Springs, then return, for a total of fifty miles. We figured that we could average nearly four miles an hour, a number pulled by me out of thin air. I figured that if an old guy

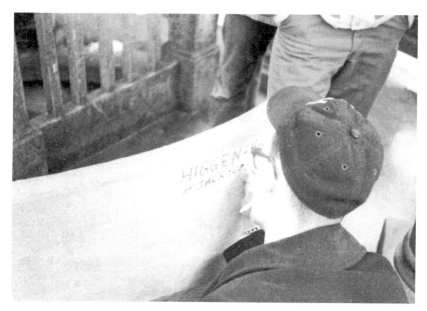

Carl Dicks at the Vicksburg Battlefield (1963)

like Bobby Kennedy could do it in eighteen hours, then surely we could do the hike faster. I assured Ron and Carl that we could do the whole thing in fourteen or fifteen hours.

The actual event proved otherwise.

We spent the night before the hike at my house, a mile of pasture from the interstate highway. We rose at 3:30 a.m. to start in the wee hours. Around my waist rested my dad's combat belt with his canteen, full. The ammo pouch carried two candy bars, a couple of Band-Aids, some toilet paper, and a small bottle of Merthiolate. My back pocket held a highway map, my front pocket some coins and a pocket knife.

I wore sneakers, but Carl wore his "boondockers." He was bound for the Navy right after high school, and he already dressed the part. He was fit and well-proportioned. Sometimes called "Cussin' Carl," he saved some of his breath for profanity, yet more for cigarettes. Carl was the only kid we knew with a tattoo, the only one who smoked. At first, he hid his habit from us, but eventually he came out—regularly rolling up a pack of cigarettes in his T-shirt sleeve. He was seventeen, but he looked ten years older, with dark stubble and receding buzz-cut hair. He had a large forehead, gray eyes, and gray glasses. He never met a dare he didn't take. Once we dared him to spray-paint a roadside White Citizens' Council sign. Carl grabbed the spray can, marched up to the sign, and did it in broad daylight, a cigarette dangling from his lips while autos passed by on Terry Road only six feet away. Whatever the project, Carl proved game. Born in New Jersey with an accent to match, his Navy parents had moved to Jackson a few years earlier. He had no use for white supremacy or segregation, instead favoring, in his own way, a "live and let live" attitude. Carl loved pool. The two of us went in to buy a used pool table for thirty-five dollars. Sometimes, we even hung out at the Twentieth Century Recreation Hall, popularly known as the "Two-Oh," a real pool hall complete with genuine tough guys.

Carl carried a canteen, a pack of cigarettes, and a Zippo lighter.

Ron wore sneakers and his usual white shirt with dark pants and carried a canteen, too. We all wore our "HH" baseball caps, which we wore with pride just about everywhere.

None of us had a watch, sunglasses, rain gear, moleskin, poles, or any other proper hiking gear. The best that could be said is that we traveled light.

The moonless dark of early morning was relieved only by starlight and occasional headlights. But the access roadway alongside our new interstate highway stretched for miles in perfect condition. We breezed along without fear of hitting potholes or patches of gravel. No one at school had yet done a fifty-mile hike. No one else was even planning one. We'd be the first. This would put us on the map. Sailing along in the dark, we surveyed half the girls in our class. Ron had news or opinions about each. Carl, who would soon have far more talent in that department than Ron and I combined, just listened, no doubt thinking something like "big hat, no cattle."

At our first water stop, we rested to do some math. The sun would be up in an hour. We figured that we'd reach the Byram exit just after sunrise. Byram lay nine miles from where we started. Excellent progress, I pronounced.

Onward.

Slowly, the sky in the east (to our left) brightened with the first gray streaks of dawn. Byram had to be just ahead, we estimated. But as far as our eyes could see, there was no exit sign. At our next break, Ron began to complain about his feet and ankles. Our canteens got lighter. We pulled out the roadmap to check the mileage, to see exactly where the Byram exit should be. Yes, I figured, we should be coming to it very soon.

By the time we cleared what seemed like another two miles and made it to the top of a rise, the sun had risen well above the horizon, and it was starting to get warm. Even in March, the bugs were out, humming. From our vantage point on top of the rise, no exit sign appeared below.

Hmmm.

At first this seemed ominous, indicating less progress than we'd thought, but I announced that we'd been making such good progress that we must have already passed Byram in the darkness. Glory be. We might make Crystal Springs, the twenty-five-mile mark, by noon. Could it be that we were moving faster than even Bobby had moved? Reassured, Ron resumed his gossip.

Finally, we saw a faint speck ahead. It had to be an exit sign. Great! What was the exit after Byram? Terry, we thought. We congratulated ourselves on approaching Terry, the fifteen-mile mark. Expectantly, we marched along, awaiting confirmation. The sun was now even warmer. Carl's eyesight rated best. Suddenly, he called upon God with great enthusiasm. Squinting, Ron and I could faintly make it out. The sign read, "Byram ½ mile." No! Holy crap! We had *not* already passed Byram. Our hearts sank.

We made the Byram exit by around ten. Nine miles down. Forty-one to go—way behind schedule. Gloom set in. We took stock. As the mathematician, I announced some findings. We were going about half as fast as I had figured. At this rate, it would take us until well past midnight to go fifty miles. We had consumed more water and grub than we should have. We had to conserve, I told them.

Recriminations began. Ron complained that I had assured them we would be home by sundown, that his body ached, and that it was all my fault. What kind of "crapola" mathematician was I?

"We can do this," I answered. "We will just have to pick up the pace."

Pace?! Ron jeered that he could not even pick up his legs.

Carl said nothing. That was his way. He never complained. He took a drag and looked at us through those horizontal slits, his thin lips turned up at the ends in a faint smile, the same "you are so full of shit" smile he had given Principal France.

All casual talk and gossip ceased. Ron's complaints morphed into wheezes. Thinking the grass might go easier on his feet, we traded the frontage road for the wide, pretty stretch of grass beside it. By the time we got to the Terry exit, we still had ten miles to go to Crystal Springs, not to mention the twenty-five-mile return trip. Salt and sun covered our faces. Our shirts smelled rank. The pain, now paralytic, Ron said, threatened his hips. Amputations were likely, he implied. Even chalking up some of Ron's catalog of woes to hypochondria, he was plainly suffering.

We rested in a copse of trees near the Terry exit for a candy bar lunch. Ron became hopeless. At one in the afternoon, we now realized that there was no way we could do the fifty miles. My own feet showed blisters in multiple places. Merthiolate did no good. To mitigate the heat, we prayed for rain, but the only clouds were faint pink-tinged cream puffs floating on the pale horizon. So, we rested—sunburned, foot-blistered, exhausted, now low on water. Could we even make it to Crystal Springs? Another ten miles? We had no choice, really. We had to. The nearest phone was in Crystal Springs. There, we could make a long-distance call to beg someone to come get us. Carl called us "chickenshits."

We resumed along the grass, which was occasionally interrupted by a stand of trees. Ron collapsed. He cried out that unbearable agony had taken hold, that his legs throbbed from toe to hip. Like the wounded guy in the war films who gets left behind, Ron begged, "Just give me a .45 and you go ahead. Leave me. Save yourselves. Don't worry about me." (We did not really have a .45—that was mere gallows humor.) But how could we leave him? One of his arms went around my shoulders, the other around Carl's. As a trio, we staggered along. This took weight off his severe blisters. The going, however, got even slower. When our feet collided, he howled in pain. Ron insisted he would walk on his own, but he could barely move.

We finally agreed that Carl and I should go ahead to Crystal Springs to call someone to rescue us; we would return to find Ron. So, Carl and I pushed on. Glancing back, we saw Ron staggering, by turns veering left, then right, then falling forward. Once we looked back, far back, to see Ron *crawling*!

If only Principal France could have seen it.

Finally, after a hard push, Carl and I spotted a gas station sign on the outskirts of Crystal Springs. We stumbled in. A pay phone! Praise be. Using almost all our coins, we called our most simpatico teacher. Calling our own houses was not a sure thing, but we could trust her to find a good soul to rescue us. We had money for only one call. She answered. We explained everything in a rush, and, bless her, she said someone would come. Relieved, we settled in the shade of a tree. Carl lit up. I used the rest of my change to buy a bottle of Coke and a bag of peanuts, each a nickel. Sweet shade, most of all, sweet rest.

But wait! On the horizon, a pitiful figure trudged toward us. Ron had found his last full measure of strength to soldier on. We hurried out to help him in. Once at the gas station, he dissolved in misery.

Ron's Aunt Bee eventually pulled up in the Mississippi Blue Streak, the name we had given her blue Chevy station wagon because of the way it streaked about when Ron was at the wheel. Ron had even had smart-ass business cards printed up announcing the Mississippi Blue Streak. But Ron was not going to be streaking anywhere for a while. Aunt Bee was a wonderful sight. She just looked at us like—how much crazier can you kids get? You dumbos, get in.

We crawled into the car. Soon we were homeward bound.

Having failed, it sure seemed like a long drive back but, God, how good it felt to ride with a song like Ben E. King's "Stand By Me" on the radio, the wind cool on our faces, seat cushions below us. In the gathering darkness, we passed the rise and copse where we had faltered. Poor Ron. His body was wrecked, he said. Forever after, through several marriages, he would blame me for the suffering in his hips, knees, ankles, and feet. I felt like a wreck, too, but recovery came sooner for me. Carl, ever the tough one, never complained. He was the only one of us who could have and would have made the return trip. This gave us a new appreciation for Carl—and for Robert Kennedy.

13

A Ride on the Rails

On Saturday, May 11, 1963, Carl Dicks, Joe Turnage, and I boarded a second-class coach on the *Panama Limited*, operated by the Illinois Central Railroad, to head for New Orleans for a day trip. The *Panama Limited* was the sister train to the *City of New Orleans*, which was destined for immortality in a few years, thanks to Steve Goodman and Arlo Guthrie. We left early in the morning and returned late that night. It took three hours each way, which left about eight hours to wander around the French Quarter, a new experience for all of us. This seemed like a good way to see the Big Easy on a low budget. We fervently hoped to find slot machines, which held our fascination. In the gambling spirit, we played penny poker all the way to New Orleans, arranged in booth-like seating that allowed two to face the third with a table in between, no doubt all of us chewing sticks of Clove gum. Trains were in decline, so we had the car to ourselves.

We found no slot machines in New Orleans. So, naturally, as a second choice, we looked for pornography. We found a porn theater (Jackson had none) playing a cheap sex movie. I'm sure for Joe and me it was a first. It proved to be disgustingly bad—an inane plot with transparent excuses for nudity and libido. Joe walked out pronto, offended by its cheapness. I soon followed, feeling it was a sure ticket to hell. Carl called us chickenshits and stayed to the end. Thereafter, we explored Jackson Square, Café du Monde, Bourbon Street, and even mounted the river levee to take in the vastness of the Mississippi. We had no alcohol, not even beer, all of us being underage. Secretly, each of us, I suspect, hoped that some worldly woman would teach us things we didn't know, but we met no women, worldly or otherwise.

Then came the most memorable part.

For a very late lunch, we went into the Woolworth's on Canal Street near Rampart. The only customers, we sat down at the counter to order hamburgers and Cokes. The pretty black waitress behind the counter smiled while taking our orders. As our burgers cooked, one of us got up to go to the bathroom. When he returned, he reported that the other side of the store had an identical counter serving white customers. There were two counters—"separate but equal"—and we had sat down at the black one.

We had accidentally integrated the black lunch counter.

Hmmm. What to do? Sit-ins at lunch counters made headlines then—but it was always the other way around, blacks sitting at white counters.

Surly-looking whites began gathering over by the gumball machines, staring at us. Maybe we'd be accosted, I worried. News cameras might appear. Maybe we'd be arrested. Meanwhile, our orders sizzled. To avoid a scene, Joe and I whispered that maybe we should take our burgers to go, but Carl nixed that idea.

"You chickenshits. I am going to sit right here and eat my goddamn burger," he said. So we sucked it up and, once the burgers arrived, did just that. Carl shamed us into doing the right thing. The store made no fuss. The waitress treated us most cordially. Some disapproving store patrons had heartburn as they stood watching, but no one made a scene. We ate, paid, then left, leaving a generous Turnage-style tip, breathing a deep sigh of relief as we stepped into the sunshine to head for the train station.

Soon, the rhythm of the rails was all that we could feel.

14

That Word

In *To Kill a Mockingbird*, set in the 1930s, Scout asks Atticus whether it was true, as she had heard at school, that he defended "niggers." Atticus tells her that, yes, he does defend them, then tells her not to use the word "nigger."

In the 1950s, the word was still in common use. Sometimes I heard it used with seething hatred, as in "Are you one of those goddamn nigger-lovers?" Other times, I heard it used descriptively, as in "Niggertown," referring to the main black neighborhood in Jackson, or as in "Young Bill, would you like a nigger toe to go with that lemonade?"—more than once a pal's mom offered me a Brazil nut in that way. The N-word had not yet acquired its modern third-rail voltage. The word was in vulgar use in much of America, as is shown in film and literature of the era.

Still, I owe it to our parents to say that they taught us, like Atticus taught Scout, that "Negro" and "colored" were polite but that the N-word was not. My mother never, I repeat never, used the N-word. My dad rarely did. Nor did I ever hear them use "boy" when speaking to a black man. Before graduating from high school, I didn't always follow their admonition. There were times that the N-word was used in our schoolyard conversations. I used it myself. The same is true for jokes about blacks. I'd be untrue to this small history to claim otherwise.

In college, our sensibilities would move in the right direction. The moral force of the civil rights movement would take hold. We would see the true indignity in the word and feel the shame of having used it. It would fall out of our usage, even in ordinary conversation, though it would continue to be a common term among the Old Guard in the Deep South.

15

'We Are for Civil Rights for Negroes'

As the civil rights movement gathered full momentum in Mississippi, our small cadre decided to speak out publicly in favor of voting rights for blacks and against white supremacy. This was just before we graduated from high school. The decision arose out of an HH meeting held, coincidentally, on Sunday, May 12, 1963, the day after our New Orleans train trip. Jackson reeled in controversy. In the weeks before, Roy Wilkins, national president of the NAACP, had come to join Medgar Evers's boycott of stores in Jackson and was arrested while picketing the Woolworth's downtown, making front pages all across America. The marches and protests continued daily. After a long discussion that Sunday, we decided to publish a letter to the editor of the *Clarion-Ledger* stating our support for voting rights for blacks but opposing other goals of the demonstrators. This letter represents a benchmark for our views on race as of mid-1963.

Our school year had begun with the Meredith desegregation of Ole Miss, our practical introduction to the civil rights movement. In the following months, names like Roy Wilkins, Whitney Young, John Lewis, James Forman, James Farmer, Fred Shuttlesworth, Stokely Carmichael, Aaron Henry, Andrew Young, Julian Bond, Medgar Evers, and, most of all, Dr. Martin Luther King Jr., had acquired household usage. We'd learned some of the differences between the NAACP and the Southern Christian Leadership Conference (SCLC), the Congress of Racial Equity (CORE) and the Student Nonviolent Coordinating Committee (SNCC). SNCC was the most confrontational, the NAACP remained the most "go-slow," and Dr. King and the SCLC hewed ever-vigilant to peaceful protest. By one count, in a ten-week period that spring, America saw 758 race demonstrations with 14,733 arrests in 186 cities.

By May 1963, the civil rights movement had become, far and away, our nation's largest domestic story. The intensity of the movement would reach a fever pitch over the next two years, especially during the Selma-to-Montgomery march for voting rights in 1965. But already it raged in 1963. During the Birmingham campaign that spring, Dr. King was arrested and, from his cell, penned his now-famous "Letter from Birmingham Jail," stating that "injustice anywhere is a threat to justice everywhere." On May 2, the Children's Crusade began, and thousands of students gathered to march into downtown Birmingham. Over the next few days, the nation, even the world, became shocked and outraged by horrific images as Bull Connor, Birmingham's commissioner of public safety, deployed fire hoses, attack dogs, and electric cattle prods on demonstrators in Birmingham, including many children.

Mississippi, too, regularly made the national news. There was the Jackson boycott, led by Medgar Evers. On May 12, leaders of the boycott sent a letter to white officials with a list of demands, including an end to segregation, but the mayor refused to meet with the black leaders. As a part of the Jackson boycott effort, a small group of Tougaloo College students and faculty staged a sit-in at the downtown Woolworth's lunch counter; they were verbally and physically assaulted by an angry mob as police looked on and did nothing. (It was during this tumult that the burning cross terrified Mother.)

By that May of our final high school year, the issue of civil rights had taken center stage with a vengeance, even among relatively sheltered white youngsters like us. We felt the issue had many moving parts—voting, desegregation of schools, desegregation of swimming pools and libraries, elimination of separate seating, equal access to public accommodations, equal access to employment, service on juries, racial intermarriage, and the freedom of store owners and employers to choose to integrate their stores and work forces. Today, most of America believes that equality trumps all other concerns—period—but in 1963, our country remained deep in debate over how far equality should win out.

While some of this came up in our Provine High classrooms, much more surfaced in our lives outside the classrooms. Almost all of us disliked being the butt of so much nationwide criticism. Our backs were up. Still, we talked it out, usually within the rough and tumble of the schoolyard. We were plainly not of one mind. A typical schoolyard argument, for example, would ask why, given that we were a democracy, blacks shouldn't be allowed to vote as freely as whites. Someone would then answer that voting should be reserved for the "educated," their premise being that blacks were uneducated. The response might then be: well, have you seen their schools? They're terrible; it's no wonder we get a better education. To which it would be insisted: no, blacks start out with equal schools but run them down. To which it would be said: no, black schools are *not* equal to begin with.

A favorite all-purpose rejoinder of the Old Guard was, "You give a nigger an inch and he'll take a mile." This was why they had to be "kept in their place." On it went. One side might, depending on how heated it got, call the other "nigger-lover" or "bigot."

We were in the centennial of the Emancipation Proclamation. The Kennedy Administration, however, had not yet proposed any civil rights legislation. Calls came from some black leaders for a march on Washington but no such march yet loomed on the calendar. Even the president's historic television address on June 11, 1963, calling for civil rights legislation remained unplanned in May. Seminal works on the civil rights movement like *Bearing the Cross* and *Parting the Waters* were still unimagined, much less published. We had no texts to consult. It's hard to imagine now, but our view of the injustice and inequality of the era was constrained and confined by the world we'd grown up in, and this consequential chapter in American history remained a work in progress, breaking all around us. So, we tried to sort it out for ourselves.

Our meeting occurred in the room above the garage at the elegant home of Joe Posey's grandparents. Joe was quiet, gentle, well-mannered, brilliant, and witty in a dry, understated way. He had an owl-like gaze with his large glasses.

We argued all afternoon. Our strongest consensus rejected white supremacy and favored equal voting rights. Our views diverged on school desegregation and public accommodations. We felt obliged to reach common ground. We debated into the evening. For our little group, the central issue was white supremacy, a cornerstone of the Mississippi way of life.

Was it right or was it wrong?

We felt it was wrong.

At our May 12 meeting, Ron Goodbread, Joe Turnage, Carl Dicks, Junior Feild, Joe Posey, and the rest of our HH group, including me, decided to speak our minds publicly by submitting a letter to the editor of the *Clarion-Ledger*. Today, a letter to the editor may seem quaint, but in those days, letters to the editor remained an important way for the public—statewide—to carry on a dialogue. The *Clarion-Ledger* did print such letters, usually against civil rights and in favor of white supremacy, but Professor James Silver at Ole Miss wrote progressive letters critical of the current system. They got published, one in the same month as ours would be. We decided to do what few whites would then do—to speak publicly *against* white supremacy and *in favor* of voting rights for blacks.*

Two weeks earlier, I had been installed as the president of our little organization. After the May 12 meeting, I composed and signed the letter with my name and address, but the letter was written on behalf of us all and captured the consensus at our meeting on Sunday, May 12. Our letter to the editor appeared in the "Voice of the People" in the *Clarion-Ledger* on June 6, 1963—D-Day, which was coincidentally also the day we graduated from high school. Our letter explained that we were local white kids and declared, "We are for civil rights for Negroes." No other homegrown white youngsters in Mississippi had ever made such a statement in print, at least in a paper of statewide circulation. I am confident this is true even though it is impossible to verify. We compared white supremacy to the Nazi creed of a master race. Specifically, our letter said:

---

* According to the attendance record, which I amazingly still have, present at that meeting were Ron, Carl, Junior, Joe Turnage, Joe Posey, Wilson Ellis, Bennett Price, and myself. Absent that day were Jack Purvis, Kitty Perry (then our only female member), Sidney Craft, Steve Haas, and Frank Whittington, none of whom, it should be added, ever dissented from our statement.

Most of the Southerners who shun the Negro and believe in white supremacy can be categorized with the Germans who once thought the Jews were to be shunned and persecuted, and believed in a master race. The difference is the Nazis have since corrected their ways.

"Corrected their ways" was a smart-ass way to say that the Nazis had been brought to heel by the victorious allies. We also said that blacks were "the whites' equal with regard to voting privileges." This was two years before the Voting Rights Act became the law of the land.

How had we stumbled upon this viewpoint? We grew up in the afterglow of the Second World War and the triumph of our parents' generation, a triumph of democracy over tyranny. In time, even our young minds wondered: Doesn't democracy mean that everyone, without exception, should have the right to vote? If all men are created equal, as proclaimed in the Declaration of Independence, then shouldn't we all have an equal say in the running of our government? Our little group thought so. But a fiction prevailed in our state. Democracy was publicly exalted, but those in power in Mississippi denied the franchise to blacks. We were in high school before "voter qualification" tests came to our attention. Even then, it took some time to figure out that they were administered via a double standard designed to pass whites and to fail blacks. When the Voting Rights Bill was before Congress in 1965, this pattern became well-documented, but in the early 1960s all we had to go on was suspicion. Nevertheless, by May 1963, our small band figured that something unfair had been going on, so we wanted to support protection of equal voting rights for blacks. In time, with a fair and equal ballot, we thought all other aspects of the race question would be worked out via a true democratic process.

Each of us came to this conclusion through a different route. In Ron's case, Abe Lincoln was his hero, so federal supremacy trumped states' rights. Joe Turnage's case had an urbane outlook, a perspective that caused him to look beyond our piney woods to the distant centers of class and sophistication. Joe wanted to believe what *those* people believed. For Danny Cupit, it was a practical sense of history with an ability to see where things were headed. For others like me, it came from the fundamental contradiction between what America had stood for in the Second World War versus what we could see happening at home, between the Declaration of Independence and the reality on the ground. Willanna's brash rejection of racism had emboldened me. Our parents had taught us to be decent and fair to everyone, and decency and fairness implied equality.

But as the entire letter itself revealed, our views didn't embrace full equality.

Dear Editor:

This letter represents the feelings of myself and the feelings of many of my friends regarding the segregation question. Our ages range from seventeen to nineteen, and all of us are of the Caucasian race. Basically here is our belief: We are for equalization in the education system of our state between the Negro and the white; We are for civil rights for Negroes, and think they are the whites' equal with regard to voting privileges; we are totally against sit-ins and demonstrations; and we do not support integration of schools and recreational facilities, and consider integration of private businesses a question to be answered only by the store owners themselves.

Our first belie[f] stated above—concerning "equal but separate" school systems—is not being upheld in the state of Mississippi, although Jackson's own system may be considered so. We therefore submit that if "equal but different" cannot be made to work, then integration is the only other alternative. Most of the southerners who shun the Negro and believe in white supremacy can be categorized with the Germans who once thought the Jews were to be shunned and persecuted, and believed in a master race. The difference is the Nazis have since corrected their ways.

The crux of the problem we believe lies in the fact that both races are wrong. The Negro believing that his general economic and social status should be improved by the Federal Government and not by himself is as wrong as the white Southerners "holier than thou" attitude. Both races will have to take another look at the problem and both races will have to make concessions. I could not say what the concessions of either race would be to make both sides satisfied; better men than I have tried for

100 years. We need in the crisis at hand the help of someone who does know the answer and are still not too old nor too intransigent to pray.

Sincerely yours,

Bill Alsup

2325 Terry Road, Jackson

JUST AS EVERYONE SHOULD have the right to vote for whomever they pleased, just as everyone should have the right to socialize with whomever they pleased, we thought that all business owners should have the right to do business with whomever they pleased, meaning they should have the freedom to integrate or not, as guided by their consciences, and not be barred by state or local law from integrating if they wished. "Integration of private businesses," we said, was "a question to be answered only by the store owners themselves." This was before the Civil Rights Act of 1964 that changed the legal landscape forever and barred discrimination in the workplace (indeed, even before President Kennedy proposed what would become that landmark law). But our view was widely held in progressive America. We, like many Americans, thought morality could not be legislated.

Although we denounced white supremacy and called for equal voting rights for all, we stopped short of denouncing segregation. In fact, we said we did not support integration of schools and recreational facilities. We didn't want a repeat of the violence of Little Rock, violence that already had erupted on Capitol Street over boycott and lunch counter sit-ins. Yet we pointed out that separate schools were *not* equal in Mississippi, and that integration remained the only alternative if the schools could not be made equal. Separate but equal had reigned as the entire rationale for maintaining segregation. Many whites claimed to believe that black facilities were in fact equal. As illustrated by the shanty schoolhouse I saw from the window of my dad's car, however, this was not so. The two systems were far from equal.

Our letter also called for understanding and conciliation between the races, opposing sit-ins and demonstrations (because they led to violence). When we wrote, "Both races will have to take another look at the problem and both races will have to make concessions," it was our stab at trying to dial down violence. Opposition to sit-ins and demonstrations was also a widely held view in America back then—the mainstream national press ran editorials calling for conciliation and talks rather than street protests that led to violence. Attorney General Robert Kennedy himself had called for a cooling-off period. The black-owned *Jackson Advocate* had urged moderation. Even the NAACP thought the Freedom Rider campaign had been unwise. We found ourselves in good, progressive company in urging moderation.

Judged by modern standards, of course, our views still had a long way to go. By the standards of 1963 Jackson, however, our letter was a voice in the wilderness.

Our little group sincerely thought we could move public opinion, especially among young whites, toward a more progressive view. We thought that true change would come on a neighbor-to-neighbor basis and via equal voting rights. By speaking out against white supremacy, we thought we could encourage others of like mind to speak up. And we wanted black Mississippians to know that at least some white kids in Mississippi wanted them to vote. We recognized that we were living through a molten moment in history. About to graduate, we wanted to make our statement while we were still together. With the idealism of youth, we thought we would lead the way.

In response to the publication of our letter, I received two Bibles in the mail, each underlined with various passages used by the old guard to support white supremacy.

16

The Murder of Medgar Evers

On June 11, 1963, the University of Alabama accepted its first two black students despite the staged "resistance" of Governor George Wallace, who eventually stepped aside when confronted (face to face) by the federalized national guard. But, unlike the chaos at Ole Miss eight months earlier, the integration at Alabama, tense as it was, happened without bloodshed. President Kennedy went on national television that very night to speak on equal justice and to tell America that he would submit a civil rights bill to Congress. That speech became President Kennedy's most important address on domestic policy. The president called for equal rights across the board, making an eloquent case for full equality. A few days later, President Kennedy sent Congress his Civil Rights Bill, a masterstroke that eventually (after his assassination) became the Civil Rights Act of 1964.

Four hours after the speech, Medgar Evers, the Mississippi field secretary for the NAACP, by then a local household name, died by rifle fire in his front yard in Jackson. We woke up to *Clarion-Ledger* headlines of the assassination. This murder occurred right in our small town, only a few miles from my home. It gave me chills but, more importantly, a strong sense of sadness. On June 12, I entered this short note in my diary:

> Medgar Evers was shot early this morning by some idiot.
> He was Field Sec. of NAACP.
> It was tragic.

Medgar Evers was a Mississippi native who enlisted in the Army, fought in Europe during the Second World War, then returned to enroll at Alcorn A&M College (now Alcorn State University), an all-black school. After graduation, Evers worked as an insurance agent. While traveling for his job, he also began organizing new chapters of the NAACP, and in 1954, he applied to the University of Mississippi law school, which rejected him. Later that year, he became the first NAACP field officer in Mississippi. He became well-known in Mississippi, as his small office in Jackson, which he ran with his wife Myrlie, actively pushed for voting and civil rights for black Mississippians and investigated racial murders like the horrific slaying of fourteen-year-old Emmett Till in 1955.

Early in the morning on June 12, 1963, after the Kennedy speech, Evers pulled into his driveway. Hiding nearby was a sniper, Byron De La Beckwith, a white supremacist. Beckwith shot Evers in the back as he got out of his car. Evers died in a hospital emergency room less than an hour later.

About ten days later Beckwith was arrested, and the *Clarion-Ledger* headline declared "Californian is Charged with Murder of Evers." Beckwith, it turned out, was born in California but had moved to Mississippi as a child. The *Clarion-Ledger* always looked for some way to place an outsider spin on every civil rights story—even a tragedy. During the trial and in view of the jury, Beckwith received a visit from Governor Ross Barnett, who shook his hand in open court. The White Citizens' Council likewise supported Beckwith and raised money for his defense. The all-male, all-white jury deadlocked. He was retried, but the second all-white jury also deadlocked. Both trials occurred in 1964. Ironically, those deadlocks registered as minor racial progress inasmuch as all-white Mississippi juries usually would have promptly, unanimously acquitted any white man accused of a crime against a black man. Beckwith was released and hailed as a returning hero in Greenwood, his hometown.*

Medgar Evers ranked as the number one civil rights leader in Mississippi. His funeral led to a spontaneous march of mourners who headed toward Capitol Street. Police used billy clubs and dogs to try to disperse the marchers, and the crowd responded by throwing bricks, bottles, and rocks.

---

* In 1994, however, Beckwith was re-tried and convicted by a biracial jury, in part based on his bragging about the murder after his release. He died in prison in 2001 at age 88.

In an act of inspired courage, John Doar of the U.S. Justice Department interposed himself between the police line and the marchers, begging the marchers to turn back and let federal justice take its course. Tension and uncertainty wracked the scene. Then, out of respect for John Doar, the marchers dispersed. Beside Doar at that heart-stopping moment stood a young lawyer, the first African American to serve in the Justice Department's Civil Rights Division, who had himself been arrested by Jackson police in the prior month—Thelton Henderson. He would, in later years, have a profound influence on me.

1963 marked a turning point for many whites in America. Before the events of that year, the civil rights movement remained suspect in white homes, not only in Mississippi but throughout the South and even beyond. After we saw brutal police tactics in Birmingham and Jackson, then the assassination of Medgar Evers, many whites paused and questioned the sincerity of those who wanted to maintain the status quo. Genteel opposition was one thing. Murder was another. What kind of people would commit these murders? Decent Southern whites, even those inclined toward segregation, asked themselves this question.

17

Class Reunion

I t's 2003 and our fortieth high school reunion. Through the crowd, I see coming right toward me the guy (now a lawyer) who angrily stood on the lunchroom table soliciting contributions to help him drive up to Ole Miss to "take care of Meredith." We haven't seen each other since 1963. He's the last guy I want to see. I wish I could just disappear. He strides up, then extends his hand, looking mostly the same except heavier with thinner hair. As we're shaking hands, he says, "Bill, you were right, and I was wrong."

18

The Summer of 1963

The summer after high school produced my first "grown-up" job. I received an offer from Sidney Ragland, who'd been my dad's partner in the power line construction business, to join a cross-country survey crew. It was an unexpected and generous offer. I said yes immediately, wanting to follow in my dad's footsteps. I had no thought of becoming a lawyer.

My first day of work found me on a three-hour bus ride to the Mississippi Gulf Coast, where all of our work would be done. The bus left from the Trailways station of Freedom Rider fame. The all-white, four-man crew picked me up at the other end. I made it five. All of us, including the field equipment, fit in an International Travelall, an oversized utility vehicle. Our summer's work would be to stake a proposed power line from Gulfport to the small town of Picayune through forests, swamps, and farms; other crews would build the power line itself later. On a typical day, we labored in the blistered, steamy landscape, taking measurements, placing stakes in the ground, tying our stakes and benchmarks into known landmarks already on the map. As the lowest-ranking guy on the crew, my job included cutting brush and felling trees (when they obstructed the line of sight), plus being a general gofer. Over the summer, I built up muscles, became even skinnier, and tanned dark. We had lunch in the field and took other meals at country cafes. No alcohol for anyone. Twice I had close calls with lethal snakes—a rattlesnake and a water moccasin. The crew saved me from the rattlesnake. I saved myself from the moccasin. At a hostel near Bay St. Louis, we all slept on army-surplus cots in a single non-air-conditioned room for a dollar per night per head. There was an outhouse in the backyard. Farther back lurked the shower house.

The crew epitomized the hard-working, paycheck-to-paycheck work ethic of the vast majority of American labor. They had a skill. They gave an honest day's work. They did it—even though the work was demanding. They were never going to be well-to-do or secure in retirement. Still, they loved America and felt blessed for the opportunity to work in a free country.

Today, my friends in Berkeley might wonder why I liked the other men on the crew when, as one would have expected, their views on race were traditional white views in Mississippi—they believed in separate but equal while I believed the equal part had never materialized. We sometimes discussed race as we cruised along in the Travelall. I made no dent in their attitudes nor did they in mine, but we all rejected violence—on that we agreed. Even though we disagreed on the larger questions, we had a job to do and sweated hour after hour alongside each other to get that job done. As Atticus tells Scout, this is our home and we shouldn't get crosswise with our neighbors because we disagree over an issue, important as it is. Differences over politics gave way to the team. They saved my life from that snake. We depended on each other. Situations like ours illustrated the human predicament in the Deep South.

THAT SUMMER, A GUBERNATORIAL primary blazed away, pitched as a referendum on Ross Barnett and the segregationists, on the one hand, versus the integrationists and the Kennedys, on the other. Governor Barnett was the racist buffoon who had stood in the schoolhouse door to block the enrollment of James Meredith at Ole Miss, leading to a riot and two deaths. His lieutenant governor, Paul Johnson, wanted to follow him into the office. (Mississippi then prohibited consecutive terms.)

In my scrapbook is a 1963 gubernatorial campaign leaflet that I picked up while working on the survey crew and have saved for all these years as a reminder how vicious times were then. It advertises "FREE shrimp and cold drinks" at a Paul Johnson rally (none of us went) and explains:

> The real issue in this campaign is for the people to decide whether or

not Governor Barnett, Lieutenant Governor Paul Johnson and the Mississippi Legislature were right in their stand against the invasion of the State by Federal troops and U.S. marshals under orders of the Kennedys.

If the people of Mississippi decide that they were wrong, and the Kennedys were right, then the backbone of all Southern resistance to integration will be forever broken and the free Elector movement, to remove the Kennedys from office, will be doomed to defeat.

If this should happen, you can be sure that the Kennedys will make an example out of Governor Barnett and Lieutenant Governor Johnson—for all other governors to take notice.

The Kennedys, the NAACP, CORE, and all of the left-wingers in America would have a celebration to end all celebrations if Paul Johnson should go down in defeat.

The rest of the survey crew liked Johnson. My diary entry for September 24, 1963, referred to Paul Johnson as a "professional idiot," then said he was running solely on what he had done to block James Meredith from enrolling at Ole Miss. "What an epitaph for Paul Johnson," I wrote. On November 1, 1963, a few days before the general election, my diary entry said merely "FREEDOM EQUALITY" in large letters, which was a reference to the general election. I was for Rubel Phillips, the moderate Republican. My diary entry for November 5, 1963, reported, "Bad news—Johnson by 80,000 votes." African Americans, of course, were denied the vote.

IN JULY, RON GAVE a "sermon" defending the Supreme Court's school prayer decision, then fresh on the books—*Engel v. Vitale* (1962), which had banned official state prayers in public schools even when pupils could remain silent or be excused. The Court ruled that such prayers constituted an establishment of religion in violation of the First Amendment. Our local churches had a practice of turning a Sunday evening sermon over to a young man (never a young woman in that era). Ron claimed to be Methodist, and he was invited to preach at the Boling Street Methodist Church in Jackson.

The school prayer decision had outraged most of white Mississippi (and surely some of black Mississippi), exacerbating resentment against the Supreme Court. The sermon at the Methodist church would be Ron at his best—giving paramount respect to our federal institutions. Joe Posey and I went to sit in the congregation to give moral support to Ron.

After the rounds of singing and prayers, Ron rose. His basic message was that a public school is an arm of the state, that the state is prohibited by the First Amendment from establishing religion and, therefore, a school could not compose a prayer to be read at the outset of each school day—even if students were able to opt out. The congregation got fidgety. By the time he was well into it and listeners could tell where he was going, half of the congregation got up to leave in disgust. Ron persevered to the end, with eloquence, to a near-empty room. This did not faze Ron, for he rather enjoyed being reviled as an outspoken critic of the status quo.

As THE SUMMER CAME to an end, I watched on television what seemed an amazing event—the March on Washington. Up to this point, almost all of the sit-ins and demonstrations in support of civil rights had led to violence perpetrated by onlookers and police. The March on Washington showed a new face of protest, namely that it could be undisturbed and peaceful, even on so massive a scale.

Mother and Sandy (1966)

On August 28, 1963, I wrote in my diary:

> Today, over 200,000 people marched on Washington. One out of
> every 900 people in America participated. It was chiefly for expressing the
> civil rights support. Viewed, as did JFK, the scene in part on television.
> Quite a crowd and the speeches were many and unvaried.

The March on Washington originated with A. Philip Randolph, founder of the Brotherhood of Sleeping Car Porters, who had proposed a similar march in 1941 but which was scuttled when President Franklin Roosevelt issued an executive order prohibiting race discrimination in employment for certain federal agencies and other companies with defense contracts. In 1963, Randolph was not going to back down again—even after President Kennedy sent his proposed civil rights legislation to Congress. Dr. King joined Randolph and other civil rights leaders in calling for the march.

The March on Washington demonstrated to a national audience that the demand for equality had wide support and was not driven simply by a few protestors. Dr. King gave his "I Have a Dream" speech (although if that was shown on our local television, I missed it). I had never before seen a march or rally so massive—and so peaceful. This was another watershed moment for my evolving views on the First Amendment and the civil rights movement.

19

A Dinner at Lalime's

It's 2013 in Berkeley at Lalime's, our favorite high-end cafe. My wife, Suzan, and I huddle close around a small table with Ann Smith Willoughby, my high school friend of the billboard chapter. For the first half hour, Ann and Suzan dissect public education and how to fix it, leaving me a little left out. It's good that they are hitting it off.

Earlier, Ann called out of the blue from her home in Kansas City, saying she'd been back in Jackson for a funeral. While there, she'd become consumed by memories of the sixties. On the phone, she asked whether I remembered "painting up that sign." I said, yes, of course. She was coming to Berkeley to visit her daughter, so we made a dinner date. Suzan, the ever-modern spouse, quickly approved, suggesting Lalime's.

Now, while these two talk, I'm thinking how superb Suzan is to entertain a strange, pretty woman from her husband's past. Also, how cool Ann is to connect with Suzan before reconnecting with me. I'm with two good-looking women, surely a boost for my stock. Scotch and wine keep coming. Life is the perfect invention.

On our second bottle of wine, we finally get around to talking about the old days. Ann now lectures all across the United States in her profession—graphic arts. In one question-and-answer session, someone had asked her what it was like growing up white in Mississippi during the zenith of the civil rights movement. She had answered with the story of the "Impeach Earl Warren" billboard. She now worries whether she had gotten it right. She didn't want to exaggerate. We relive that moment and compare notes. I remind her of the photo of our paint job in the Jackson Daily News and of the names they called us. "You should have told that audience," I say, "that you turned out pretty well for a one-worlder." She is proud, I can tell, that she made this small mark on the right side of history back then. "Oh, yeah," Ann smiles, "what was a one-worlder?"

20

Get an Education—
the Ticket to Somewhere

In Mississippi in 1963, the question for us as we left high school was not, as it would be for many in the next generation, where to go to college, but whether to go. Most adults felt lucky to have a high school diploma. Our dad had grown up on a farm in the Texas hill country. When he finished high school, he wanted to go to Texas Tech but the Great Depression dashed that. Instead, he learned surveying and engineering in the Work Projects Administration and later in the Army Corps of Engineers. He earned a civil engineering license simply by passing the state test (with flying colors), a college degree then being unnecessary in Mississippi (which was one of the reasons my parents chose Mississippi, I suspect). Mother, also raised on a Texas farm, had a nursing degree from a two-year college in Texas. Time and again, both drilled home this message to their kids: *Get an education—it's the only way to get anywhere in life.*

Willanna became the first in our family to enter and to graduate from a four-year college, in her case Mississippi State College for Women, the oldest public college for women in America, more commonly known as MSCW or "The W." So, on the question of whether to go, because of Willanna's example and parental exhortation, I always assumed my answer would be yes. When I was about thirteen and incorrigible, my dad once wondered aloud, in a generous moment, whether I might go to West Point, which made me think it was a reformatory. By the time I figured out what West Point was, he had died, so that idea went nowhere.

Dad passed on to me his intuitive knack for the mechanical arts. At fifteen, for example, I theorized, then proved, while resting in bed one afternoon, that combination padlocks should have *two* combinations, not just the given one. Playing with a Master combination lock that afternoon, I imagined how it must work on the inside—the internal wheels with notches that had to line up for all three wheels. I further imagined that if that were so, then you could line up the notches going left-right-left rather than the usual right-left-right, using different numbers to account for the thickness of the inter-wheel tabs. Instead of a given right-left-right combination like 30-10-0, for example, you would use 22-14-0 with the opposite left-right-left sequence, assuming that the inter-wheel tabs were one unit in width. (The tabs, in fact, may be slightly off from one unit to the next.) On my first try, it worked! No lie!

Math and science had been my best courses, so I decided to follow in my dad's footsteps to become a civil engineer. I applied only to Mississippi State, the agricultural and engineering college, which accepted me and even gave me a small scholarship (since I was a National Merit finalist with good grades). Between the scholarship and a VA stipend (received as a result of the war-related cause of my father's death), MSU was affordable. Tuition was $125 per semester. All other expenses came to less than $1,000 per year. Also bound for MSU were Junior Feild, Sidney Craft, Joe Turnage, Jack Purvis, and almost all of our HH organization. Ron Goodbread won a full scholarship to Millsaps College in Jackson, the best academic institution in Mississippi. In fact, all of the HHers except Carl enrolled in college (and graduated).

Although I went to Mississippi State expecting to become a civil engineer, two experiences during the next four years would direct me toward a career in law. One would be the civil rights movement and its echo on our rural campus. The other would be advocacy and the MSU debate team. In parallel, two experiences in college would reshape my attitudes on the race issue. Again, one would be the civil rights movement with its ever-mounting moral force. The other would be the student YMCA with its voice of conscience.

LOCATED AT STATE COLLEGE (near Starkville) in the undulating farm country of northeast Mississippi, MSU began in 1878 as a land-grant college under

Me at my ham radio station, all pre-transistor vacuum-tube gear (1963)

the Morrill Act, signed into law by Abraham Lincoln during the Civil War. Its first president was Stephen D. Lee, a Confederate artillery officer (a distant cousin to Robert E. Lee). There were 7,000 students enrolled in mid-1963, 94 percent male, no blacks. State College was a two-hour drive from Jackson, so it was close enough to visit Mother and Sandy about twice a month. Although MSU had few women students, 2,200 women enrolled at the nearby Mississippi State College for Women in Columbus, twenty-two miles away, where Willanna had studied and Sandy would eventually go. The narrow two-lane highway between MSU and MSCW would be bumper-to-bumper every weekend night.

Unless there was a football game on campus or it was exam time, the MSU campus seemed dead on weekends. On a typical weekend, about three-fourths of the student population went home while most of the rest went visiting at MSCW. On Sundays, though, the cathedral-style cafeteria still would be full at the noon hour due to the custom of nearby Starkville residents coming there for "dinner" after church. The cafeteria put out its best menu for that occasion. Starkville persons of color, however, were officially not welcome.

ON SATURDAY, SEPTEMBER 7, 1963, Junior and I hopped into his white 1960 Oldsmobile to drive to MSU, excited as hell. After the two-hour drive, the first thing we did was get our room assignments, both, as it turned out, in Hightower Dorm. I drew Room 236 with Joe Turnage. Junior drew Room 324 with Sidney Craft, our neighborhood classmate since grade school. It might seem odd that Junior and I didn't choose each other as roommates, given how long we had been friends, but Junior and Sidney, with athletic scholarships, were both bound for the MSU baseball team (and two SEC championships). Unathletic, Joe and I talked big about debating and paired up.

The next Monday began with orientation for all 1,200 entering freshmen. We stood in a lot of lines, first on the sawdust floor of the agricultural exposition arena leading up to various card tables to sign for our class assignments. There, we had to take a math test. I got a perfect 40 for 40, after having detected a repetition in the sequence of multiple-choice answers. (What use was made of those tests remains a mystery.) The late summer simmered oven-like—no air conditioning. Sweat trickled down our faces and inside our shirts. Quickly, we had to choose between the line for Army ROTC versus the line for Air Force ROTC. One or the other was mandatory for all incoming males. More of us, including me, chose Air Force ROTC so we wouldn't have to carry or clean a heavy rifle. Jack Purvis and Frank Whittington, two of our HH group, got in the Army line.

It was campus tradition that new MSU males had to have their heads shaved, then wear dumb-looking "beanie" caps. My head got buzzed (at an outdoor stool surrounded by mounds of hair) but the embarrassing beanie was worn only rarely. All males had to strip down at the infirmary, then "spread your cheeks," draftee style—part of the drill to see how healthy we were. We acquired cowbells, required to be rung in celebration of all touchdowns. It all felt like a cross between a state fair and a boot camp. We had become Bulldogs, the school mascot.

By the prominent rust-brick YMCA building in the middle of campus,

Me, Joe, Junior, and Jack as ROTC cadets in our freshman year (1969)

ancient oaks cast a pleasant shade over yet another card table. The line at this table led to a sign-up for the YMCA, which most everyone did (including me). The campus Y prevailed as the equivalent of a student union. The post office and a pool hall took up the basement of the Y building. A large bulletin board hung outside the post office. Hundreds of notes sought or offered used books, slide rules, even rides.

In the sweltering heat, still another line formed at the bookstore, then tucked under one end of the cafeteria. I checked off my list. Later, with armloads of books, mechanical-drawing gear, slide rule, tablets, and uniform, I found my way back to the freshmen quadrangle, dumped it all on my bed, then sorted it out. That evening, our Provine High contingent headed back up the long hill from the dorm to try out the cafeteria. Another line, but hey, no sweat. We felt only excitement, adventure, pride—with a healthy dose of anxiety.

The male freshmen quadrangle occupied a large flat treeless lowland at an edge of campus, a single cluster of four identical three-story dorms, each shaped like a boomerang with the arches bent in toward each other. Each dorm floor had a single bath-shower at one end and, at the other, a single rotary pay phone bolted to the wall. The phone could be cheated if you dropped the nickel in and simultaneously hit the change-return plunger just right, which would return your nickel while still giving you a dial tone. On Friday evenings, a line grew for the phone, almost always desperadoes hoping for last-minute dates. No one had a phone in their room.

On the ground floor, the dorm commons room fell in the middle of the building's boomerang shape. A twenty-inch black-and-white television stood up front. Via an antenna and analog signal (no cable), we received CBS, NBC, and ABC with varying degrees of fuzz on a cathode-ray tube set that took time to warm up. The chairs got arranged theater-style to maximize viewing. Around suppertime a couple of dozen would gather for the national news—then only fifteen minutes in length. Walter Cronkite had recently become the CBS news anchor. Walter became the nation's number one newscaster and, as it also happened, the nation's number one cheerleader for the space program.

Each small rectangular dorm room had two single steel-frame beds with thin mattresses on squeaky springs, a built-in-the-wall desk long enough for two to work side by side, tiny closet space for two with drawers, a single sink under a mirror, a flimsy towel rack, and one window. On hot nights, it proved best to sleep with your door open so the huge fan at the end of the hall could pull more outside air through your window. The desk was set into the wall with plenty of shelves above for books and pads. I drew the bed and desk nearer the window, Joe the bed and desk nearer the hallway.

Joe and I had thought we would be great roommates. *What a mistake!* We loved each other dearly—still do today—but we proved incompatible from day one. He was an unrepentant night owl. I was an equally unrepentant morning person. My brain went soggy at 10 p.m. That's when I went to bed to manage a 7 a.m. calculus class every Monday through Friday. (On Saturday, I had an 8 a.m. class in something else, so thankfully I could sleep an hour longer.) Joe seemed biologically unable to start studying until eleven. He played poker down the hall, then returned late to do his homework. Or, he stayed out until eleven when he would return to "get ready to get ready," as he phrased it, for study. He needed the light on. Then, doing homework at his desk, he mumbled audibly to himself as he solved math problems. This went on well past midnight.

Worse, Joe, the suave one, went out for the fraternities. I did not. I didn't want to give them the satisfaction of rejecting me. Junior and I and most of our crowd remained GDIs, which stood for "Goddamn Independent," and we were proud of it. So, at the outset, Joe stayed out every night for "rush," then "pledge." Unsuave, alone in the room, I did my homework, shut off the light, then turned in around ten. Around eleven, to repeat, Joe burst through the doorway, flipped on the light, to exclaim, "Deal 'em," or "Gamble, gamble, gamble."

Bless him, we finally worked out a *modus vivendi*. He would sneak into the room late at night (while I slept), leave the overhead light off, then crawl under a tent-like shroud, made from a sheet, tacked around his desk. Then he would snap on his lamp. The shroud blocked most of the light. This made it easier for me to remain asleep. If I woke up, which happened now and then, I could see his shadow silhouetted against the tent and could hear his murmur. But it became dimmer, quieter. Joe reported that it got hard to breathe in there. He had to come out for air. Then he would go back under to tackle more equations. He became a prince. He endured the shroud until the end of our freshman year. Then we got a divorce—as roommates but not as pals.

My very first course proved to be my favorite—calculus with Professor Wayne Gaddis, all of that year. In the dead of winter it was dark outside when class began at 7 a.m. Through the third-floor windows of Lee Hall, perched on the highest part of campus, we could see the cold landscape light up as sunrise broke. We sat in those old wooden desks with half of a desk top on the right side, tattooed with initials, dates, and other carvings. The building had ancient, clanking radiator heat. Water and steam pipes ran along the tall ceilings. The walls were plaster, the lights incandescent. The chalkboards were black, not green. Lee Hall had been built in 1910 and had hardly changed.

Mr. Gaddis, a tall, Lincolnesque farmer, drove a pick-up. No nonsense. No small talk. His creased middle-aged face told of hard times. He wore a short-sleeved shirt with a tattered tie. He always arrived ten minutes before class to chalk a calculus problem for the day's lesson onto the blackboard and started class exactly on time.

One morning, some beefy football players in the class huddled in earnest just as the lesson was about to start, debating the difference between "real" and "imaginary" numbers, a finer mathematical concept. Seeking to sneak in the question before proceedings began, one of them asked, "Mr. Gaddis, we have a disagreement here. Is zero a *real* number or an *imaginary* number?"

Chalk still pinched in his fingers, Mr. Gaddis momentarily turned from the blackboard, bent slightly forward, focused on his questioner.

"Son," he answered in earnest brilliance, "I've had zero dollars many times and it's real."

Like almost all classroom halls, the old McCain engineering building remained wide open all year, at all hours. In the warm months, the windows also stayed open day and night. Most of the engineering and drafting courses occurred there. Anyone could go in, take a seat to study, even at midnight. No one worried about crime or theft or the electricity bill. Once, Joe and I studied there for a final exam until the wee hours. With chalk scraping and clacking on the old blackboard, we worked out the math for a cannonball trajectory, taking into account air resistance. Many nights during exam periods I'd hunker down in a classroom, usually as high in a building as possible, to study all alone, often until ten o'clock, even midnight, settling into my lonely drill—systematically working through every possible problem that might be on the exam. Even before college, I had worked hard on math and science, but at MSU I immersed myself. The main difference was my dad's death. At times, I felt his presence in those lonely rooms. I yearned to make him proud.

21

MSU Debate

One thing Joe and I shared—we wanted to be able to stand on our feet and make a convincing argument. We wanted to debate, and we wanted to shine.

The new MSU debate coach was Thomas Brad Bishop, who arrived on campus at the same time we did. Brad came from Alabama, and he was all of twenty-four years old. He had been a football player in college, earning a degree in speech. Now, in the fall of 1963, he moved his new family to nearby Starkville to teach speech and coach the debate team. Brad was built like a fire hydrant, stood about five-nine, and looked more like a football coach than a debate coach. He talked slowly and distinctly—in complete sentences—with a perfect Southern drawl (though he insisted that we pronounce "Mississippi" correctly rather than skipping over the second vowel). He could not help breaking into a smile, even when he criticized someone. He anointed himself "the Big Dog," meaning, we gathered, that he led as the big dog, and we followed as the pups. He was boyishly handsome and had snagged a brilliant blonde wife, Anne.

Joe and I showed up early for the organizing meeting in Room 10 of the YMCA after dinner on Wednesday, October 2. A total of seven prospects arrived. Two were returnees from the prior year. One returnee was Dorothy "Dot" Leatherwood. With perpetually flushed cheeks and cat-eye glasses, Dot was a tall, thin brunette, a senior. She loved debating and was fearless. She had one speed—full tilt. Dot was the first "coed," as women students were then called, whom I met at MSU. The other returnee was Kirk Shaw, a junior from the small town of Newton. Kirk, who became known as the

"Newton Nice Guy," had the gift of being able to boil a problem down to its essence, arguing from common sense rather than a stack of "evidence" cards. He exuded confidence and candor. A master of the rhetorical question, he would tilt his head slightly to ask in a kind but authoritative drawl, "Wouldn't it be better to try a less drastic alternative before committing so much . . ." completing the rest of the sentence to fit the occasion. He preferred to make one solid, irrefutable point rather than diluting his time between two lesser arguments. Kirk and Dot had debated together the year before. They paired as partners for our year, too.

Joe and I stayed the course while all other newbies fell by the wayside. Together with Kirk and Dot, we were four, enough to field a pair of two-person teams, the bare minimum for tournaments, never minding that the schools we went up against had twenty to thirty debaters. The tournament topic that year was whether the federal government should guarantee an opportunity for higher education to all qualified high school candidates. We'd argue the pro for half of any tournament, then the con for the rest. During our first year, we traveled to regional events in Jackson, Birmingham, Hattiesburg, Ruston, Columbus, Houston, and Macon, among others, all in the Deep South. Mother opened our home to the team for the Jackson event. Dot and Kirk, our powerhouse duo, racked up wins. Joe and I had a poor start but overall did okay by year's end.

We had a budget of only six hundred dollars for the entire year, so Brad practiced frugality. The drill was simple. We piled into Brad's Rambler, two in the front with three in the back. We usually left after sundown, drove all night to avoid the expense of a motel, and arrived by the next morning at the tournament. We changed into our debating clothes at a gas station or in a washroom at the college. When we had to stay overnight, Brad would go into a motel, unannounced, to bargain for a "student" or "educational" discount. When he came up short, we'd try elsewhere. He stretched our six hundred dollars a long way.

In early 1963, a few months before we arrived at MSU, all hell had broken loose when the MSU basketball team wanted to accept an invitation to the NCAA championship tournament in Louisville, Kentucky. Because MSU would have to play against racially integrated teams, the state board overseeing our colleges emphatically forbade MSU from accepting the invitation. While the politicians opposed it, the players favored accepting the invitation. One player told a reporter that he had grown up in cotton country and had played basketball with blacks all his life. MSU President Dean Colvard, decent and quietly progressive, adroitly defied and outwitted the board and the governor to get the team to the tournament. MSU lost to Loyola University Chicago and its African American players, who went on to win the national championship. Still, for MSU, that tournament became history.

Thanks to that precedent, or at least following it, we debaters competed in integrated tournaments. Our first one was the Mississippi Youth Congress in the fall of our freshman year. We used the real Mississippi Capitol for mock legislative proceedings. Ron came, too, representing Millsaps. Joe, Ron, and I proposed a bill to outlaw voter-intelligence tests, one of the gimmicks then used to deny African Americans the right to vote. We had considerable support but got out-maneuvered, losing the battle. (At the next year's event, however, the same bill succeeded.) On a separate front, true to credo, Gambler Joe sponsored a bill to legalize a state lottery, which went down in flames but made the front page of the *Clarion-Ledger*.

Tournament events were judged by coaches from other schools. In all four years, the best comment I ever received from a judge came at that first Mississippi Youth Congress. After one session, the judge approached me. She was African American, a coach for a black college in the competition. After her specific suggestions on my performance, she said, "Someday you are going to be a United States senator." That compliment, a small, no doubt long-forgotten moment for her, was a long-remembered inspiration for me.

On the debate team, we learned to do more than construct an affirmative case. We needed to anticipate what the other side might raise in opposition, then construct the rebuttal. Doing this suggested ways to streamline and improve the affirmative case by eliminating nonessentials that merely invited easy attacks by the other side. This seems obvious now. It was easy, however, to give short shrift to the other side's possible arguments when we were preparing. We learned the hard way to anticipate them fully. So we worked at test-driving our various scenarios. Using straight-talking responses to the other side's arguments, we could see wins play out in the tournaments. Throughout my legal career, this basic lesson would prove invaluable.

The quantity of evidence mattered less than the convincing force of the evidence. As Kirk showed us, one solid well-developed point beat two half-baked points every time. In later law practice, however, I would see that most litigators cling to even their weaker points, wanting to throw "everything they have" at the other side. Good trial lawyers, like the one Kirk would become, do what Abe Lincoln did as a trial lawyer—concede multiple points to get cleanly at the one point on which they cannot lose.

22

A Blood-Soaked Miracle: The Civil Rights Act of 1964

On a Sunday morning in mid-September 1963, only a few days after we arrived at MSU, a bomb exploded in the Sixteenth Street Baptist Church in Birmingham. Four girls were killed.

The church had served as a headquarters during the intense desegregation campaign and historic marches held in Birmingham during the spring of 1963. Everyone suspected that the Klan had bombed the church as a reprisal. Birmingham Public Safety Commissioner Bull Connor blamed the Supreme Court. Deep South propaganda claimed that as tragic as these deaths were, liberals and civil rights advocates had asked for trouble by trying to change the established Southern way of life.

Yet, this atrocity—the murder of four precious children—may have done more than any other single event to cause white Southerners to stop, to think, and to focus on racial injustice in Alabama and Mississippi. Even in the Deep South, decent whites condemned the murder of those children, and decent whites were ever more uncomfortable to find themselves on the same side as the Klan in resisting integration.

Two months later, on Friday, November 22, 1963, I worked alone in the commons room in Hightower Dorm, repairing an old upright piano I had retrieved from a curbside junk heap. The dorm mom had let me park the relic there in the commons room. I concentrated on unsticking a key. Clear northern light flooded through the window to my right. It was midday. My classes were over. Many students had left for the weekend. Nothing was on my mind other than the mechanics of a stuck piano key.

The dorm mother emerged from her small apartment off the commons room and approached me, appearing shaken. At first, I thought my tinkering with the piano bothered her, but something about her face told me otherwise. Her voice could barely summon the words: "They're saying something about the president being shot." She became frail, confused. Her apartment door remained open. I could hear her television. She'd been watching a soap opera, she said, when it'd been interrupted by a terse news bulletin, but then it cut back to the regular programming. We went back into her small apartment and stood before her television. The soap opera continued. For a couple of minutes, all seemed normal. Then, the television screen froze on "CBS News Bulletin" while a network audio announcement said that word was coming from Dallas about three rifle shots in an attempted assassination of President Kennedy and that the regularly scheduled programming would be interrupted for updates. The soap opera returned but was soon interrupted again. Walter Cronkite appeared in his white shirt sleeves in the CBS newsroom in New York, his demeanor most serious. During the next twenty minutes or so, he reported that President Kennedy had been shot by rifle fire during a motorcade in Dallas, that his companion, Texas Governor John Connally, had also been shot, and that both were at Parkland Memorial Hospital.

Perhaps Kennedy would be able to survive it well enough to serve out his term. That was my first thought. I clung to this hope until we were told that a priest had been called. Then I feared the worst of the worst.

Finally, Cronkite delivered the awful report:

> From Dallas, Texas, the flash apparently official, President Kennedy died at one p.m. Central Standard Time, two o'clock, Eastern Standard Time, some thirty-eight minutes ago.

Cronkite removed his glasses in shock and respect, pausing, as he held back tears. Then, the consummate professional, he resumed with the important responsibility to tell America the news as it broke.

The dorm mother and I remained standing through it all, in stock-still silence, stunned. She'd lived through the Great Depression and Franklin

Roosevelt. The presidency, I have no doubt, ranked as a matter of reverence for her. For me, it deserved respect. JFK had guided us through the Cuban missile crisis. He'd been a war hero. I admired him.

Others did not. As we watched that small screen, we could hear something outdoors through the open windows by the piano. We could hear the ringing of cowbells, the MSU way of celebrating. What was being celebrated? Through the window, we saw dozens of students outside running around at random, whooping with glee, ringing their cowbells as if a touchdown had just been scored. We then realized that they were celebrating the assassination of our president. This broke my heart. Hers, too, no doubt. Cowbell celebrations erupted all over campus that day, we eventually learned. This became one of the harshest memories of my life.

I went home to be with Mother and Sandy to mark those four indelible days. Bearing the unbearable, our First Lady led us through it, all televised in grainy black and white, with remarkable grace and unmatched strength.

On that Friday, I wrote in headline block letters in my diary (adding the last sentence a few days later):

PRESIDENT KENNEDY ASSASSINATED IN DALLAS BY SUS-PECTED CUBAN SYMPATHIZER. WORLD SHOCKED. LBJ SWORN IN EN ROUTE TO WASHINGTON WITH BODY IN JET.

I was working on piano in dorm when housemother informed us.

The Saturday entry:

Gov. Conn[a]lly of Texas will be OK. The assassin was supposed to be a marine reject Cuban sympathizer 24 years old named Lee Harvey Oswald. Body taken to Washington yesterday. Casket closed. It will not be opened.

The Sunday entry:

Assassin shot by Dallas nite club owner today as he was being moved to county jail. He died in Parkland Hosp across the hall from the room in which JFK died Fri. A policeman was killed trying to capture Oswal[d].

The Monday entry:

> President Kennedy laid to rest in Arlington Cemetery. Millions watched it on TV. 1 million watch[ed] it in Washington. Very pompous. John Jr. saluted his father's casket when it was being buried.

By "pompous," I meant rich in ceremony and protocol. Those diary entries have stood the test of time and seem reasonably accurate more than half a century later.

Almost as hard was the fifth day, the Tuesday after the assassination, on the MSU drill field. Our commander-in-chief had fallen in the line of duty, but our AFROTC officers completely ignored the loss and made us march about with no acknowledgment—not a single word—of the tragedy.

I penned a tribute to our late president and asked Ron, our HH newsletter editor, to publish it.

> Despite our nation's recent loss of the future wisdom and guidance of an able leader, the country is not left without legacies; our nation has not lost his acts of courage, nor his deeds of just and common good, nor has it lost the result of his striving to support America's ideals embodied by its Constitution.
>
> For the example John Fitzgerald Kennedy as an American leader, as an American soldier, as an American citizen and as a faithful Christian—for the mark he left upon world history and for every gift of God, Americans may thank Him we have been so blessed.

Was the president killed over the race issue and his clarion call for civil rights progress? At first, I wondered if that had been the reason, but when the facts came out, it seemed clear that the assassin had been a delusional loser, a Marxist Fidelista bitter about America and his lot in life. He had acted alone, his twisted way to leave a mark on history.

On November 27, the day before Thanksgiving, President Johnson stood before a televised joint session of Congress to call upon legislators to enact the Civil Rights Bill proposed by Kennedy, saying that would be the best way we could remember the fallen president. Thunderous applause greeted this call. It became a rare instance of a united national will. The country yearned to remember President Kennedy. So, with terrible irony, one good thing, the pursuit of the Civil Rights Act of 1964, eventually came out of our horrific loss.

Our new president vigorously pushed the Kennedy Civil Rights Bill. Because of his legislative expertise (having been the Senate majority leader), LBJ found ways to navigate the system. In January, the House passed it, but when the bill arrived in the Senate, it was beset by filibusters, and debate on the bill continued for sixty days. Beginning on June 9th, Senator Robert Byrd of West Virginia read an eight hundred-page speech for fourteen hours and thirteen minutes (still a record). Breaking the filibuster fell to Republican Everett Dirksen, a gravelly voiced, chain-smoking, wavy-haired senator from Illinois, the Land of Lincoln. As the ranking minority member, he had been enlisted by Majority Whip Hubert Humphrey and Minority Whip Thomas Kuchel, at the urging of LBJ, to help them gain the Republican support necessary to end the filibuster. Dirksen then spent months adjusting the bill in order to maintain its crucial substance while making it more appealing to the Senate minority. Finally, the amended bill was ready, and Dirksen spoke before the vote to end the filibuster. Lincoln and the Emancipation Proclamation no doubt on his mind, Dirksen invoked Victor Hugo and said, "Stronger than all armies is an idea whose time has come."

President Johnson signed the bill into law on July 2, 1964. My diary entry for that day simply said:

> Civil Rights Act of 1964 signed into "Law of the Land" by President Johnson.

Only a miracle could have gotten the act through. The miracle came as a result of four things lining up at the same time. The first, as mentioned, was the fortuity that President Kennedy had already proposed his Civil

Rights Bill before he was killed. I say "fortuity," again, because he had pro-posed it in June 1963 *against* the advice of his top aides. The second was President Lyndon Johnson. He vigorously pursued the Civil Rights Bill and had, by virtue of having learned every trick in Congress, the unique skill (and forcefulness) to work around all the legislative roadblocks. The third was Everett Dirksen, who worked tirelessly to gain the Republican votes needed to break the filibuster. The fourth, and very consequential, factor was the moral imperative of the civil rights movement. Throughout all of the violence perpetrated against activists, marchers, protesters, and ordinary black citizens going about their lives, even after the Sixteenth Street Baptist Church bombing and the murder of four young girls, the civil rights move-ment remained peaceful, thanks in large part to Dr. Martin Luther King Jr. By mid-1964, public opinion in America had shifted to favor reform.

My own attitude had been that just as all Americans, including blacks, should have the right to vote for whomever they pleased, so, too, employ-ers and proprietors should have the right to serve or employ whomever they pleased and that the choice of whom to serve and whom to employ should remain a moral, ethical question for each employer or proprietor to answer for themselves. I thought that decent employers and proprietors would choose, in time, to include all, black and white. The Civil Rights Act, however, answered that moral question as a matter of law for the nation as a whole. Discrimination in the workplace and in public accommodations was over. I accepted that judgment. The country had debated it at length, finally made a decision as the law of the land, and that decision ended the question of segregation as far as I was concerned. Democracy had spoken. Now it was time to make it work.

But many whites in Mississippi vehemently opposed the Civil Rights Act. It was the Freedom Summer—hundreds of college students from the North came to Mississippi to advance the cause of voting rights (which the new law didn't cover). In late June, just two days after the Senate voted to pass the bill, three civil rights workers disappeared in Neshoba County, Mis-sissippi. As the search wore on, ultimately bringing more than two hundred FBI agents to Mississippi, and the young men were not found, the world feared that they had been murdered. Nothing else could explain it. The bodies of James Chaney, Michael Schwerner, and Andrew Goodman were finally discovered in August, buried in an earthen dam near Philadelphia, Mississippi.

It was shameful to take in that horror, all the worse for it happening in Mississippi, our home. Many whites regretted the murders, and some even wanted the murderers to fry in the electric chair, me included, but a large number of whites in Mississippi were not sorry, just as many had celebrated Kennedy's murder. In the summer of 1964, Klansmen or their ilk burned or bombed dozens of black churches, homes, and businesses, and beat more than eighty civil rights workers in Mississippi—in addition to the murders of Chaney, Schwerner, and Goodman. Those three didn't live to see the Civil Rights Act signed by LBJ in July. They were killed, I felt, because it had finally been passed, just as, a year earlier, Medgar Evers had been murdered within hours of President Kennedy's announcement that he would send a Civil Rights Bill to Congress.

Violence wracked Mississippi. I abhorred the murders, the bombings, the beatings, but felt unprepared to take action. Simply having good will toward racial progress was all, I thought, that decency required. I was willing to let the long, slow arc of justice take its time. It would be two more summers before I would even flirt with the movement.

MEANWHILE, WE WERE LIVING through an explosion of historic music—rock and roll, the Beatles, and country revival. For two dollars a head, Johnny Cash and June Carter performed to a sold-out crowd in Lee Hall on May 6, 1964. Sensational! I got their autographs on the ticket, still in my scrapbook. Later that night, Cash was arrested for public drunkenness and spent the next six hours in jail, leading to his song "Starkville City Jail." Those two brought the house down.

But far and away, folk music carried the day. The best and most historic of all such concerts proved to be a solo performance by Joan Baez at Tougaloo College near Jackson on the Sunday evening of April 5, 1964. Tougaloo was the preeminent black college in the state, a crossroads for the civil rights movement. Being Mississippi's biggest Baez fan, Danny Cupit (soon to become my roommate) attended that evening, as did many

Millsaps students, among a statewide audience. Also in the audience were undercover investigators from the State Sovereignty Commission (whose reports, we later learned, reviled it as an "integrated" event drawing many automobiles "with out-of-state tags"). Student admission was $1.50 at the door. To the integrated audience, Baez said, "If any of you are going to get kicked out of school for having your picture taken in the audience, you'd better change seats." Danny didn't want to move from his near front-row seat but his friend was afraid to have the magazines take his picture, lest his local-cop dad find out he had attended, so they moved to the rear. At the end, Baez led the audience in "We Shall Overcome." This event was said to have been the most integrated event ever held on the Tougaloo campus.*

There have been times in our history when our nation's songs have been more important in expressing the national will than our nation's laws. The civil rights era became one such era. The laws had proven inadequate for the task at hand—indeed the laws had proven unjust, like mandatory state segregation. But songs of the era expressed what America in its conscience knew was right. "We Shall Overcome" is now most remembered, but other memories include "Oh Freedom!" and "This Little Light of Mine." In time, they became anthems. And, eventually, our laws followed suit and gave way to federal statutes of historic proportion.

THAT SUMMER OF 1964, I had an epiphany of a different sort. I returned to the survey crew. The first summer I had been a bush-and-tree cutter and general gopher. The second summer I got promoted to "instrument man" because the usual transit operator had been drafted. The "instrument man" rated as a good position—mostly mental, with little bush-and-tree cutting. I had to level the transit directly over a pin in the ground, then "turn the angle" (precisely) using a traditional mechanical transit resting on a wooden tripod. Sometimes advanced trigonometry was required. I got a small, much-needed raise. I really liked the work.

This set the stage for a curious but memorable life-changing moment.

---

* Joe and I missed out on this gem. As members of the MSU debate team, we had left Jackson at 5 a.m. that morning to drive to Houston for a tournament. Danny had not yet joined the team.

With the survey crew in the summer of 1964

One day, we had to "take a shot" across a swamp—that is, to extend our survey line straight across a wide water body into the soggy ground beyond. (You can't drive stakes into a water body.) We had to take the shot before the heat waves built up, for heat waves would have introduced error by causing the range pole, as viewed through the transit, to appear to jump left and right. So, we rose early one morning before sunrise to hike into the swamp, arriving there at six. I set up the tripod and transit at the edge of the already-staked side of the swamp while the others marched around it to the unstaked, far side, a quarter mile away, with the range pole and other equipment, a long circumnavigation and thus a long wait.

As I was waiting, a powerful thought suddenly formed in my mind, out of the blue.

"You do not," it said, "want to do this for the rest of your life."

I replied quietly, "No, I don't."

In that moment, I crossed a Rubicon. As much as I liked the crew and the work, I realized that it wasn't my calling. It seemed strange because I hadn't been worrying about career choices. To repeat, I liked running the transit and loved my job, especially the outdoor part. My first year at MSU in civil engineering had been good to me. But that "voice" became one of the strongest feelings I'd ever had. I knew immediately that it was right. Curiously, though, it did not tell me what I *did* want to do the rest of my life.

When the summer was over, I went back to MSU and veered off in a new direction—aerospace engineering, a hot ticket in those days. It would be another year before I heard the call of Atticus Finch.

23

Danny Cupit

Now it's time to meet Danny Cupit, the friend who attended the 1964 Baez concert at Tougaloo, and with whom we'd together find the courage to take a stand against the system. As new roommates, we moved into Room 106 of Sessums, a second-year dorm, his prior roommate having had an annoying tendency to sleepwalk. By this point, Danny had tried out for the debate team, so we'd become good friends. At least once in our freshman year, we'd hitchhiked to MSCW in Columbus in search of dates. We would remain roommates until we graduated in 1967.

Danny's dad had an eighth-grade education and worked a blue-collar job for the *Clarion-Ledger*. Danny had been the center on our state championship football team at Provine. Muscular, he was broader than most of us but not overweight—he was just tough—and no chicken when it came to fistfights. At the wheel, he'd cruise around with his elbow out the window, taunt tavern lowlifes with wisecracks, and place the rest of us in the car at risk of a rumble. He had light brown hair and blue eyes. Like my mom, his was a superb cook. Danny enjoyed food. Near the end of meals in the cafeteria, he would survey our plates for any unfinished food and often ask something like, "Are you going to eat that roll?" In high school he'd been an average student, but in college he tried for good grades as a business major. He spoke mostly in phrases, rarely in sentences, and never in paragraphs. Debating helped change that.

Danny and I proved compatible as roommates. We both turned in around ten, a window cracked for fresh air, no matter how cold it got. We both hated frats. We both liked supper at the same time (early), so we regularly went to the cafeteria together. Our politics converged. We had no bad habits. With respect to women, our luck ran about the same (below average).

Practical jokes prevailed in our crowd. The Electrocution Stunt topped them all. In Sessums, the switch on my bedside lamp was frozen in the "on" position. To turn it off, I had to unplug the lamp. To turn it on, I had to plug it back in. Danny had observed this pattern and knew that every night I would plug it in to read in bed. Danny, Joe, and Junior wrapped thin wire around the electrodes of the wall plug on the cord for my lamp. As ten o'clock approached on the night in question, I pulled the covers over me and reached for the plug, totally oblivious to their prank. I wondered why they were huddled in the corner farthest away from the metal-frame bunk bed, as they pretended to talk about some dumb item in close quarters. I inserted the plug into the wall socket. Ka-bam! Sparks, smoke, even molten metal exploded—with my hand, of course, still pushing on the now-flaming plug, my arm vibrating from hand to shoulder in the sharp, jolting manner of an electrocution. Simultaneously, the lights went dark building-wide. With each vibration of my arm, the lights flashed on and off like a strobe. With each flash I could see those three hunched over in convulsive laugher. The plug was burned beyond recognition. I survived. Danny said Joe and Junior made him do it.

24

Our Condolences to Charles Evers

As 1964 drew to a close, Danny and I decided to go visit Charles Evers, brother of the murdered Medgar Evers.

Just after midnight on June 12, 1963, as described earlier, Medgar Evers, a husband and father, was shot and killed in his front yard in Jackson as he came home late from an NAACP meeting, a few hours after President Kennedy's civil rights address.

Evers's NAACP office in Jackson was a simple cinder block building on Lynch Street, about four miles from our house, near Jackson State College for Negroes (as it was then known). After Medgar Evers was buried with full military honors in Arlington National Cemetery, his brother Charles took over the leadership of the Mississippi field office. President Kennedy brought Medgar's widow, Myrlie, and Charles to the White House where he told them, "You know, they'd kill me, too, if they could." Charles Evers had stood only a few feet from Dr. King during his "I Have A Dream" speech and was, even before the assassination of his brother, a noteworthy figure in his own right.

One of our few liberal teachers at MSU, Flavous Hutchinson, felt his days at MSU were numbered and wanted an appointment to the United States Court of Appeals for the Fifth Circuit. He happened also to be a loyal national Democrat. Danny took a course taught by Professor Hutchinson, and they became friends. On the evening of Tuesday, December 15, according to my diary, I, too, talked with Professor Hutchinson about his plans to become a judge. Danny and I both wanted to help. I smile now over the notion that two sophomores in college could influence the filling of a federal judicial vacancy, but we thought that even the least help was better than none.

While home over Christmas break at the end of 1964, Danny and I decided to go to the NAACP field office in Jackson to meet Charles Evers. We wanted to promote the idea of Professor Hutchinson for the federal circuit court and—truth be told—we wanted an excuse to introduce ourselves to a real civil rights leader. With no appointment, we just dropped in. The office was near where my mom had encountered the burning cross. Local white kids didn't often walk down Lynch Street, much less drop into the NAACP headquarters. We felt self-conscious out on the sidewalk and even more so as we entered the small reception area. A courteous black woman greeted us in subdued tones. We explained that we were local boys and wondered if we could pay our respects to Mr. Evers. She disappeared into the next room. Danny and I remained alone in the small reception area— simple linoleum flooring, posters, bulletin-board items, magazines, ashtray stands, and serviceable chairs. No one else was in evidence. A huge poster of Medgar Evers hung on the wall, along with pictures of Dick Gregory and Robert Kennedy. The woman returned to say Mr. Evers would see us, then escorted us into his office.

In the dimly lit room with the curtains drawn, we could see more plain cinder block walls, a large desk with two chairs in front of it, and a new, red carpet. Papers piled in disarray covered the desk and every other flat surface. On the desk a worn wooden nameplate read "Mr. Evers," referring, we assumed, to his brother. Charles Evers politely shook our hands, but we could tell that he was wondering "Who in hell are these white boys, and what are they really up to?" I wouldn't have blamed him if he'd had a handgun at the ready. He offered us seats and remained behind his desk. We told him we were born and raised in Mississippi, that we were very sorry for the loss of his brother. We wanted him to know, we said, that not all white Mississippians opposed civil rights for blacks. He took this graciously.

He asked more about us. We said we were Jackson kids at MSU. We then told him that one of our two true liberal MSU professors—Flavous Hutchinson—would make a great appointment to the federal court of appeals. We thought it would help to have black leadership support our candidate. Mr. Evers had never heard of Hutchinson but thanked us for the idea and wrote down the name. We also asked if he would be willing to help us by giving a speech at MSU. Of course, this was big talk for two young kids. We didn't know yet that the state authorities would never allow a black to speak on a white campus. He replied that, yes, if we got him an invitation, he could probably do that.

He gave us a phone number. He said that if we phoned him, we should be aware that all phone calls in and out of his office were tapped by the FBI, so anything we said would likely be recorded. I was taken aback by this for a couple of reasons. The idea of wiretapping scared me. Worse, I had thought that the FBI was on the side of civil rights activists and that we only needed to worry about the Mississippi police. This proved not to be true, as FBI history has since revealed.

Back on Lynch Street on an overcast winter afternoon, Danny and I strolled down the sidewalk, excited over what we'd just done and over whatever we were getting ourselves into.

Actually, we didn't have any idea what we were getting ourselves into. We knew we lived in a rotten system, but it was the system in which my mom and Danny's dad had jobs, the system in which we'd been raised. Maybe in some as-yet vague way, we could help nudge progress.

Charles Evers would eventually speak at MSU but not on the timetable we wanted, as we shall see. He went on to serve as mayor of Fayette, indeed to become the first black mayor in Mississippi since Reconstruction (thanks to the Voting Rights Act), to campaign for Robert Kennedy, to run for governor of Mississippi as an independent in 1971 (unsuccessfully), and eventually to switch parties and become a Republican.

25

Another Miracle:
The Voting Rights Act of 1965

The Civil Rights Act of 1964 was hardly written into the law books when, after his landslide victory over Barry Goldwater, President Johnson proposed the Voting Rights Act. Voting and Selma then became relentless headlines. This unfolding drama captured my attention, so I made a number of diary entries. I was nineteen. In the dorm commons room, I watched the president's speech, then wrote the following in my diary on March 15, 1965:

> [I] Saw LBJ on live TV tonite ask Congress to pass a voter laws bill to protect Negro voters from discrimination. Once, near the end, he said, "...and we shall overcome." He did not meet with warm reception. Many foul-mouthed passers-by in the lobby.

The latter reference was to students in the dorm commons area who disapproved of voting rights for blacks and uttered nasty comments as the president spoke. I then believed (and still believe) that LBJ genuinely and fervently wanted racial equality. Two days later, I wrote:

> LBJ sent his Voting Bill to Congress today. It was reported by Congressman [Thomas] Abernethy in the *Clarion-Ledger* that Americans were [de]frauded Mon. nite because the TV showed alleged congressmen applauding the President yet ½ of Congress was gone and most of the people showed were executive staffers, officials and even pages dressed to the occasion. I truly believe however that such legislation with modification is needed.

The Mississippi propaganda machine reported that during the president's speech the House of Representatives was somehow staged to project counterfeit support for the bill.

The Selma to Montgomery March for voting rights in Alabama was actually three events over the course of three weeks, the first one notoriously stopped in its tracks with billy clubs and tear gas at the Edmund Pettus Bridge in Selma. On March 22, the second day of the final march from Selma to Montgomery, I wrote:

> Selma to Montgomery March started as led M. L. King, Jr. Varying between 300 and 4000 strong. Will last four days. Fed. courts have OK'd the march.

By the time marchers reached the Alabama capitol in Montgomery on March 25, they numbered closer to 25,000. On March 24, Attorney General Nicholas Katzenbach testified in support of the Voting Rights Act, and my diary entry reported:

> Attorney General Katzenbach today testified before a Senate Subcommittee that it would take under existing [federal] laws, six to ten years for Negroes to vote in Alabama and Louisiana. He made no estimate for Mississippi. The quote from the CBS Evening News brought cheers from the redneck audience at MSU's Sessums' Dorm lobby as thirty or more packed in to see the recent developments on the Selma march. Early this p.m. (Thurs.), Joan Baez, Peter and Paul and the Freedom Singers entertained the marchers protest[ing] in front of the Capitol in Montgomery, Alabama.

Again, that reference to the local reaction—that is, applause for the idea that it would take blacks so long to register to vote—seems incredible today, but back then it was common fare. My own view anchored itself to a fundamental faith in democracy. Reform would provide the vote to all. In turn, full and fair balloting would, I believed, solve almost all other race issues. President Johnson signed the Voting Rights Act into law on August 6, 1965. With its provision of federal registrars, it had a swift impact in Mississippi.

26

National Contenders

Danny Cupit had never tried debating before he joined us at the beginning of our sophomore year, but he proved to be a natural (and would become one of the most successful and admired attorneys in Mississippi). Danny was particularly good when he was indignant, like when he caught the other side fabricating "evidence" or pulling some other dirty trick.

To illustrate the whole of a superb debate year, a single story answers. In the spring of 1965, we received an invitation to a national debate tournament at Pacific Lutheran University in Tacoma, Washington, sponsored by Pi Kappa Delta, a national forensic society; we were card-carrying members. More than three hundred teams would be competing. The annual topic was whether the federal government should establish a national program of public works for the unemployed, yet another topic still worthy of debate today. To raise money for the trip we went door-to-door selling hundreds of boxes of peanut brittle. Given that our team had so far had a strong year, the school then found another thousand dollars for the trip. Dot Leatherwood had graduated mid-year, so I got paired with our quarterback, Kirk Shaw. Joe and Danny became partners.

We had the best road trip of all time. In early April 1965 we beamed in a photograph, holding a "Tacoma or Bust" sign, that ran in the *Clarion-Ledger* over the headline "Unlikely Quartet Eyes Trip"—"unlikely" because we were long shots to place at the tournament, coming as we did from a backwoods venue. Danny's dad, who worked in the press room at the statewide paper, had helped arrange the publicity as an occasion to use its new full-color photo equipment. A few days later, we waxed the "Big R," Brad's

Rambler, then loaded it. Early the next day, we five climbed in, closed the doors, turned the key, and headed west.

We cleared Starkville, then Mathison, then Winona, and finally felt we were on our way when we came around a hill and there stretched below us was the flatland of the Mississippi Delta, "the most Southern place on earth," as Professor James C. Cobb has called it. On our moonless first night, I drove, nervously negotiating narrow roads in the curvy Arkansas hill country. The Big Dog's plan was "to hump it" to Flagstaff, meaning we would drive straight through to Arizona without rest, saving money and time. This meant taking turns at driving while others tried to sleep. Being in the middle of the back seat, straddling the transmission housing, proved the hardest for sleeping, so usually that guy, the driver, and the navigator talked while the other two slept against the back windows. The coach professed to have a "bad hip" that prevented him from "riding the hump" in the back seat.

The plains of Oklahoma lit up as dawn broke on Route 66. Our only chance to stretch our legs came at diners or gas stations. We crossed the Texas panhandle—relentless flatness. The smell of oil permeated the air. Next came the dry air in New Mexico. We felt like cowboys. At a windy roadside picnic table in the desert, we made sandwiches. The bread turned to toast before the first bite, the air was so dry. The mesas and sage thrilled us. At sunset, with me on the hump, Joe drove us into Albuquerque while Danny sang "El Paso." It was the wrong town and the wrong voice, but it fit perfectly. Later that night, I slept against a back window, then thrilled to wake with wonder at spying snow on the ground. In the darkness in Arizona, we stopped, just to check. Sure enough, it *was* snow. A freezing wind had swept the high country.

After our first rest in Flagstaff, Brad and Joe wanted to get to Las Vegas. Joe, our gambler, had swapped driver's licenses with a friend old enough to play in the casino. Their general descriptions matched (this being before picture IDs). While on the road in the back seat, Joe memorized *Scarne's Complete Guide to Gambling*, mumbling various card combinations and probabilities to himself. In Las Vegas we checked into the Dunes Hotel, got our usual two rooms for five guys, then gathered for a night on the town. When we piled into a taxi in the porte cochere, the driver said, "Where to?"

We felt like cowboys—me, Joe, Brad, and Danny in New Mexico en route to a national tournament in Tacoma; Kirk took the picture (1965)

Danny said, "The Strip," whereupon the driver said, "You're on it, Mac." So uncool. Joe was mortified. Eventually, Joe played blackjack for hours. His fake ID worked perfectly. With no fake ID, I could get away only with playing the slots but won five dollars on the last nickel of my five-dollar gambling budget.

Finally, after seeing Los Angeles and and touring San Francisco, we arrived at Pacific Lutheran University. They put us in dorm rooms. The magnitude of the challenge now sunk in. We had enjoyed big publicity back home. The school had given us extra money to cover expenses. We had played hard on the long road trip. Now, it was time to stand and deliver.

Each debate ran an hour, and each debater went to bat twice per debate (fifteen minutes total per debater). The tournament lasted three-and-a-half days. When Kirk and I walked into a contest room, typically a classroom, we could sense our opponents, usually from top tier schools, feeling they would walk away with the round, anyone from Mississippi already having a strike against them. However, after Kirk introduced himself as "Shaw, Kirk Shaw," and after he began to perform, demolishing their drivel, we could sense the momentum going our way. Kirk was our heavy hitter. All I had to do was avoid errors.

Teams did not know their wins and losses until the end of the tournament. At the awards ceremony, we were shocked—and ecstatic. Kirk and I had won seven debates and lost one. Both of us earned individual "superiors." We came in second out of hundreds of teams (from 133 colleges and 29 states). Kirk deserved the credit. I got reflected glory. Joe and Danny won three and lost five; their record would soar skyward before our college years ended.

We enjoyed one social outing arranged by the tournament, a salmon bake on a tribal island in Puget Sound. Filets were roasted over hot coals, all very tasty, my first salmon ever. We took a ferry both ways. On the way back, two young "coeds" from Iowa approached Danny and me. In turn, this led to a heartfelt conversation about race attitudes in the South. They had rarely met or seen a black person, given the demographics of Iowa then. They burned with curiosity about Mississippi and what it was really like. This led to one of them pairing up with Danny and one with me on the evening boat trip back from the island; it was as close as Danny and I came to female adventure on the whole trip.

A FUNNY THING HAPPENED on the road trip home. We "humped it" all the way from Tacoma to Reno. *Scarne's Guide*, Joe's gaming Bible, came back out, for Joe could not wait to gamble again. All the way from Tacoma, he again immersed himself in probabilities and strategies. Even in the darkness, I could tell Joe was reciting the odds tables to himself. We crashed at a Reno motel just before sunrise, tired as hell. Again, it was five guys in four beds in two rooms. Joe and I drew the short straws, so we shared a bed. I fell asleep in a flash, but Joe kept moving around in bed. Soon, however, I sensed that his half of the bed was empty. I rolled over, saw steam from the shower hanging from the ceiling with Joe before the mirror, fully dressed in his dark gray "Maverick" suit, the one with the vest. He was brushing his silky blonde hair, bending closer to the mirror to check his part.

"Joe," I asked, "what the hell are you doing?"

"Gamble, gamble, gamble. Time to get up," he grinned, continuing to primp.

"It's only 6:30 in the morning," I replied. "We've just gone to bed."

"No," he insisted, "it's 6:30 *in the evening*, and we've slept all day."

"No, no," I repeated, "it's 6:30 *in the morning*, and we just got here."

We looked out the window, and I declared, "See? The sun's just coming up."

Still adjusting his hair, he replied suavely, "No, it's just going down. We've slept all day. Deal 'em."

Cupit came to life. Irritated, he agreed with me that it was still morning, then told us to shut up. Joe thought we were tricking him. He became positive that he'd slept over twelve hours, not just a few minutes. Finally, the two of us agreed to settle it by going next door to ask the coach. With me in shorts and T-shirt and Joe in his Maverick suit, standing out in the cold gray light, we knocked on the coach's door.

Eventually, Brad opened the door, sleepy-eyed, also in his shorts and T-shirt.

"Yeah? This better be good."

"Coach," Joe asked, "is it 6:30 in the morning or 6:30 in the evening?"

He looked at us in disbelief, like we were pulling a stunt. "You assholes. Go back to bed," he said, slamming the door.

Crestfallen, Joe undressed, then crawled into bed.

Soon enough, he got his gambling fix in Reno and had another run at Vegas (he claimed to have broken even on the trip). Then we humped it home.

27

The Coolest Place on Campus

O ver the summer of 1965, I decided to become a lawyer rather than an engineer. That, I now think, is what the voice in the swamp was trying to tell me the summer before. Two influences had been at work. One was our success in debating. I liked advocacy. Even on a national stage we had held our own against the best schools. The other factor was the civil rights movement and the public-policy role that lawyers were beginning to play. In June 1963, President Kennedy had called upon the law profession to provide volunteer *pro bono* representation to civil rights workers in Mississippi and throughout the South. This quickly led to the formation of the Lawyers' Committee for Civil Rights, one of the stellar organizations to emerge from that era and one that still performs outstanding service today. By the end of 1963, volunteer lawyers came to work in Mississippi. They put a new face on an old, hidebound profession and promoted the idea that lawyers could be an engine for doing good. Atticus Finch, even though he was a fictional character in *To Kill a Mockingbird*, inspired me to believe that even a small-town lawyer could stand up for something right. I wanted to become Atticus. That December of 1965, I explained the choice this way in my journal: "Upholding fairness is a noble calling."*

At first, I planned to go to law school with an aerospace engineering degree but, after another semester, even that plan would change. To benefit from more liberal arts courses, I eventually switched to mathematics, in the

---

* That summer, on August 9, 1965, I stopped making daily entries in my diary and started making occasional entries in a journal, the idea being to describe items of interest in more detail (but less frequently).

college of arts and sciences rather than the college of engineering. Almost all of my engineering credits transferred toward the math degree.

Letting go of engineering was a tough decision. My dad had been an engineer (and he got there the hard way—with no college). More or less, I understood that occupation and what it would be like. No one in our family, however, had ever been a lawyer or had even gone to a four-year college before Willanna. MSU had no career counselors. We were left to sort out these cosmic questions on our own. Mother felt both career paths would be superb and that I should follow my heart. I had no grasp of the structure of the law profession but took it on faith, like Dickens's optimistic Micawber, that something would turn up. I decided for law. Within a few months, I'd learn that Danny was thinking along the same lines.

A SECOND MAJOR TRANSITION that summer was moving into the YMCA dorm, which turned out to be the coolest place on campus to live and, more importantly, proved to exert a distinctly progressive influence.

The stately red brick and white wood YMCA building dated back to 1914. Back then, the college received a grant from John D. Rockefeller Jr. (whose long life ended only three years before we arrived at MSU). The grant stipulated that the building be forever used for the social and religious purposes of the students—perfect for the YMCA program already underway on campus. Every aspect was built to double strength.

We had often gravitated to the YMCA in the dead center of campus near Lee Hall and on the highest crest. The State College post office and the pool hall filled the basement. After dropping by to pick up mail, most of us would linger in the pleasant shade or walk up the wide outdoor staircase to the massive front porch of the Y or continue on through its tall screen doors and stroll into its expansive lobby, which offered a television and stuffed easy chairs. Off to one side of the lobby, warm light glowed from the glass doorway of the office of the director of the Student YMCA. On the other side were a large corner "boardroom" and, beside it, Room 10, a smaller conference room, where Brad had held our first organizing meeting for the debate team. Tall double doors led to the YMCA auditorium that could hold four hundred.

At the outset of our sophomore year, I noticed mysterious stairs going up from the lobby. What was up there? One day I went up to see. I found twelve dorm rooms. I was gently ushered out but learned that twenty-four male students roomed there and that you had to apply and be accepted as a dorm resident. The landlord was the Y, not the school administration. Wow! I told Danny. We immediately knew the Y dorm was the ticket! But how could we get in?

Near the end of our sophomore year, I won a campus-wide election for vice president of the student YMCA cabinet, the governing board of the Y program. I had been drawn into the Y orbit through service on one of its committees. Danny Cupit and I applied to room in the Y.

We got in!

Danny worked in Jackson that summer, but I stayed on campus for a summer job, so the Y let me move in right away in June 1965.

Jack Purvis and I roomed together that summer. Jack was skinny with dark eyes and hair. Jack had arrived on Colonial Drive a few years after Junior and became a Higgen Hog pal. In high school we had gone in together to build a four-wheel vehicle out of two three-speed bicycles welded into a frame powered by two discarded lawn-mower engines. It went thirty miles per hour, had a rod to steer the front wheels in parallel, and bicycle brakes for stopping. We called it the "Hubba Hubba Special."

Danny returned to campus in the fall of 1965, and we resumed as roommates (Jack then moved in next door with George Verral). The YMCA dorm rated better than a frat house. Every two rooms shared a single bathroom, almost like having your own bathroom. Danny and I shared with Coleman Chong and Garland Robertson. They had the corner room facing the front of the building, while Danny and I had the corner room facing the rear. Being in a corner, our Room 210 had windows facing two directions. Through the rear window (facing north) we could see all the way down to the freshman dorms half a mile away. Our side window (facing east) looked out under a canopy of nearby trees onto the old infirmary. Danny took the bed parallel to the rear wall, and I got the one parallel to the side. We had radiator heat but no air conditioning. With double-strength walls, we had quality quiet for study and, for fun,

*The campus YMCA at Mississippi State University (2015); the windows
at the upper right framed my desk in Room 210*

Danny's scratchy old mono record player, dedicated to Baez and Dylan.

Being in the center of campus, unlike most of the dorms and all of
the frats, saved time going to and from class or to and from the cafeteria.
Our friends found it convenient to drop by between classes, so Room 210
became a hangout. The oversized porches also became a pleasant place to
sit and watch the world go by.

In Room 210, Danny and I prepared our lessons and prepped for
debates as before, but more importantly we talked our way through the
twists and turns of life. As I put it in my journal in 1967, "Sometimes at
night with the cold wind rattling those windows on the hill," we lay awake
in the darkness and examined "issues in Mississippi, the world, girls, our
friends," occasionally getting so tickled that "we would fill the dark room
with laughter." Room 210 also became Ground Zero for progressive campus
politics. There, we would eventually work our way through the Mississippi
Speaker Ban and what, if anything, we could or should do about it. There,
we hatched the Mandate for Change, a campus political reform movement.
There, we imagined the possibility that one day we might be law partners.

28

Setting the Stage

During our junior year, the stage became set for the controversy that would define our college years. Helping us set the stage was the Reverend Cermette Clardy, a most progressive influence. He arrived in the summer of 1965 as our new faculty director of the Student YMCA program. A United Methodist minister in his early thirties, Cermette wore a collar for sermons and a tweed jacket at work. He handled a pipe but never seemed to light it. Thin and fit, a jogger years before it was cool, he stood medium height with closely cropped brown hair. His gray-blue eyes smiled. He'd gone to college at Wofford and divinity school at Emory, both ivy-covered enclaves of enlightenment in the South. His politics leaned pro-civil rights, we eventually gathered, but this was not advertised as such; otherwise, he would never have won the job. Rather than being a firebrand, he preferred dialogue and the Socratic method to lead us to think again. In our conversations, he dropped Reinhold Niebuhr, an influential theologian who had just received the Presidential Medal of Freedom. Cermette's charisma drew students into the Y program. His crowd—our crowd—would hang out in his office or in the commons room or on the porch. Guitars, most welcome. Acoustic only, please.

Cermette and I met as he was settling in and taking stock. He and his wife Anne set up house in nearby Starkville. Their very first purchase was a window air conditioner, so oven-like was that summer. Although he was to have an enormous impact on many of us, his first year became a time to plant seeds. The Student YMCA had never been a politically active organization. Under Cermette, it shifted more and more in that direction. His ecumenical brand of Christianity, simply put, gradually came through—involvement in the world as it is while expecting to make it better, just as Jesus would have done. As a new officer on the YMCA cabinet, I was likewise finding my way. Eighteen months later, I would write in my journal that Cermette had "changed my life and attitudes faster than anyone else."

What exactly did that mean? We came to MSU as students to learn and to launch our careers. To get anywhere in even the regional economy, we knew we needed to study hard and to learn a skill. We had no trust funds or friends in high places to fall back on. Learning became all-consuming. Even debating remained a sideline. When it came to the larger issue of civil rights, our responsibility, we assumed, was simply to have a thoughtful, considered belief and to be of good will. Through subtle redirection and dialogue, however, Cermette encouraged us to go a step further—to *act* on our beliefs, more than that, to *act* together, *i.e.*, to organize. Like Professor James Silver, Cermette believed (but never said outright) that "men of good will" were not enough. The times required action, responsible action, but action nevertheless. Cermette thought, as did James in the Bible, that we should be doers of the word and not just hearers. Yes, we were still just kids. From our remote campus, of course, we couldn't right the major wrongs in Mississippi. But Cermette helped us eventually see that we were in a position at least to address some of the wrongs on our own campus, among them, the suppression of controversial ideas.

WHILE THE YMCA BUILDING itself dated back to 1914, the YMCA student organization dated to 1882 and had continuously been the main student organization on campus. It had long promoted games, competitions, speeches, Christmas events, and other endeavors for students. Fees came from a small charge collected from members via the university. Today, the MSU Student Union is the main student organization, but in the sixties that entity was still an infant and its role was in transition.

I sat on the Y cabinet as the vice president. We met in the board room, a corner conference room with a large oak table and room for sixteen, plus extra chairs along the wall. Our meetings always opened with a prayer, which was traditional, but Cermette's prayers trended more modern. They

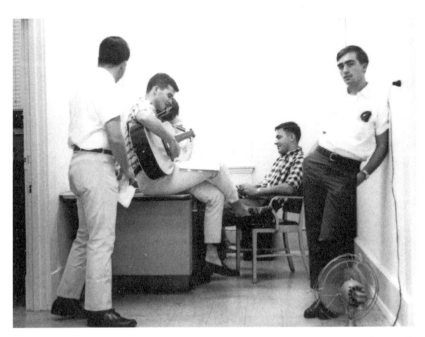

Me with guitar hanging out in Cermette's office at the YMCA with Frank Whittington (left) and others (1966)

suggested what we might do rather than for what we should be grateful. Our programs continued with the usual features, such as an orientation for freshmen; receptions for foreign students; a leadership conference; a seminar on love, courtship, and marriage; and—something new—ecumenical programs suggested by Cermette.

As a portent of stonewalling to come, the all-powerful dean of students refused to let us invite Thomas Altizer to speak on campus about his book *Radical Theology and the Death of God*, which had made the cover of *Time* magazine that year. The reason for the rejection: he was "too controversial." We acquiesced without appealing to MSU President Dean Colvard. As a substitute, the administration let us invite an uncontroversial theologian, a more colorless academic, to speak on the general subject. He came and droned on. We had other lyceum programs as well that year, but few stirred excitement. Our chapter of tumult waited, still a year away.

Cermette and the Y program became the crossroads for a distinct minority of the student body and faculty critical of hidebound racism in Mississippi. We could sit on its fine old porch with a pal or hang out in the lobby and comfortably compare notes. Cermette's charisma attracted young minds from all over campus, not just from the Y dorm. In *Maroon and White*, an excellent history of MSU, Professor Michael Ballard writes that "the YMCA seemed the one exception on campus where there could be anything approaching student activism."

The YMCA and Cermette also seemed to attract women students. The Y's gravitational field quickly introduced me to many more MSU women than I had met in my first two years. Consider three examples, all of whom were pioneers in their own right, given how few women then enrolled at State.

Camilla Wilson, from Corinth, had no trouble finding the Y right way. She had a built-in homing device for kindred souls. Her politics verged on radical. That was not, however, immediately apparent. She seemed a delicate Southern belle who loved laughter. She was Olivia de Havilland with the steel of Emma Goldman. She showed the best of Southern manners. Never, for example, did she say "shut up" when a "hush up" and a smile would do. Camilla loved Harper Lee's *To Kill A Mockingbird*, published in 1960, and we swapped favorite passages while rocking in the chairs on the grand front porch of the Y.

Two years behind me was Debbie Davis. Debbie grew up in a military family and had lived on bases all over. She'd spent summers in Aberdeen, Mississippi, where her mom had been raised. At the beginning of her first year at MSU, we met during the YMCA orientation for freshmen, sitting together on the bus ride to the orientation camp. Tall and thin, she remained quiet and observant, taking it all in before saying much. In time, she would become a leader on the debate team and within the Y and eventually would be elected the YMCA's first woman president.

Susan Eiland, a year behind me, had been at MSCW but hated the elitism of the social clubs, so she transferred to MSU, discovered the Y crowd, then felt at home. She was firmly against the Old Guard and the entrenched white power structure. She saw the Y group as an oasis in a cultural desert. She was thin with smiling eyes, the kind that are usually thinking of something playful. At least once, Susan sneaked up the stairs to Room 210. She

wanted to see Ground Zero. Her family lived out in the country on a large
farm near Macon, about thirty miles from MSU. They invited me over for
a memorable Italian dinner one Sunday (her mom was Italian). That afternoon, Susan took me down to her grandmother's old house, which was
elsewhere on their land. It was an old two-story antebellum, from which
earlier Eilands had left to fight for the Confederacy. She gave me a tour
inside. It remained just as her grandmother had left it, furniture and all, a
1930s table radio, an old gramophone, a museum of life from a bygone era.

A HISTORIC EVENT OCCURRED that summer, and the YMCA took on a sup-
porting role. In July 1965, Mississippi State University admitted its first
black student. Richard Holmes grew up in nearby Starkville, the foster son
of Dr. Douglas Conner, the founder of the local branch of the NAACP.
After beginning his college career at Wiley College in Texas, Holmes decided to seek a transfer to MSU, which, after all, was his hometown college.
President Colvard, who had proven to be a progressive moderate, found
a way to admit Holmes without the violence that had shamed Ole Miss
three years earlier. In the spring of 1963, as mentioned, Colvard had boldly
sent the MSU basketball team to the integrated NCAA championships over
the objection of the white establishment and particularly over the vitriolic
protests of Governor Ross Barnett and M. M. Roberts of the state college
board of trustees. On the enemies list as a result, Dr. Colvard would soon
be recruited away as president of UNC-Charlotte, but in the sweltering
summer of 1965 he got Holmes peacefully admitted to MSU. Dr. Colvard
steered Holmes's enrollment into the summer session to minimize attention
and arranged for Holmes to live initially at home in Starkville rather than in
a dorm. No riot. No protest. No General Walker. No violence. No deaths.
Governor Paul Johnson kept silent, eating his words from the gubernatorial
campaign of 1963, no doubt influenced by stronger federal laws and the
realization that he already had enough blood on his hands. (Meanwhile,
back at Provine High, my sister Sandy prepared to be part of the first racially
integrated class in Provine history, also peacefully accomplished.)

Thanks to good leadership by Dr. Colvard, we avoided violence at MSU.
Nevertheless, when the campus refilled in the fall, Holmes initially got the

cold treatment from most students—and even from some faculty. Holmes was the only black person in a sea of white faces, students and faculty alike. Once, Susan Eiland saw him sitting alone in the busy student union and sat down to talk with him. This small act of kindness led to mean-spirited rumors in her hometown of Macon.

At the YMCA, Cermette proposed that we welcome Holmes and make it clear to him that we were supportive. To that end, Holmes was plainly welcomed at the Y, its program, and our building. The YMCA's warmth toward MSU's first black student had a lasting effect. By the early 1970s, "the Y building had become a sort of unofficial gathering place for the black students," according to John K. Bettersworth's history of MSU, *People's University: The Centennial History of Mississippi State.**

ANOTHER CIRCUMSTANCE THAT SET the stage for the drama of our final year was our success for MSU on the debate team, experience that taught us how to make good arguments. Tournaments also exposed us to progressive attitudes of other students all over the country. That year, the debate topic was whether law enforcement agencies in the United States should be given greater freedom in the investigation and prosecution of organized crime.

Joe and Danny continued as one team. With Kirk graduated, my new partner became Scott Wendelsdorf, a year behind us. With a medium build, blue eyes, and short brown hair, Scott had a crisp and to-the-point style. His politics seemed radical. And he was irreverent and funny as hell.

We embarked on another grand road trip, this time to compete in Harvard's fabled tournament. Our first stop was Washington, a first for all of us. At Arlington Cemetery, we paid our respects at President Kennedy's gravesite, then still a fresh, simple grave (instead of the granite monument we know today). We toured the White House, the Supreme Court, the Capitol, and the Smithsonian, then mingled with the college kids in Georgetown, all in a snowstorm. It remained bitterly cold—the dead of winter, the whole time.

Next came Manhattan, another first. We met with Turner Catledge,

---

* Although Holmes and I met in the Y, and he was always welcome in Room 210 (Junior recalls meeting Holmes in Room 210), one of my MSU regrets is that the two of us never became friends.

managing editor of the *New York Times*. He was an MSU alum, so the meeting had been arranged through the school. We met in his ample office. He said that when he had been at MSU, he and Ben Hilbun, later a president of MSU, had been debate partners. They had argued for the proposition that teachers in Mississippi should have at least a high school education. Mississippi College, however, beat them with statistics showing that there were not enough high school graduates in the state to make the plan work. A *Times* photographer captured our visit, showing Danny leaning forward, LBJ-style with his chin cradled in his hand. As we left the *New York Times* building, an anti-war protest filled Times Square. "Vietniks" planned to lie down in the streets. Two hundred policemen waited for them. Many protesters were arrested. We could not yet envision the number, the very large number, that would take to the streets to protest the Vietnam War by the end of the decade.

In Manhattan, we'd originally checked into the City Squire Hotel at Broadway and 51st. When a massive blizzard blocked all roads out of the city, we couldn't leave town, so we needed to save money. To that end (and to be more hip), Danny, Scott, and I moved to the Hotel Earle near a corner of Washington Square in Greenwich Village. This ranked as a true dive. The "tariff sheet" specified a daily rate of four dollars for two in a "room with running water (share a bath)." We got a large room, with fractured windows, that never warmed up. We went down to ask for hot water and heat only to learn that the desk clerk had just been shot. The lobby was crawling with cops. From the Earle, I wrote Mother, "Last night at the Hotel (Rattrap) Earle, we froze our ass. This a.m. we hardly could make it out of bed. The wind rattled the windows all night. I felt this a.m. like I do after camping out."

Finally, the freeways were plowed enough for us to leave Manhattan—just in time, for after one more day we would have missed the tournament in Cambridge.

The Trolley Track Incident occurred as we reached Cambridge—Country Boy meets life in the Big City. We made it to Harvard Square in the middle of a huge late-afternoon wintry traffic jam. Total gridlock. We noticed that an exit on our righthand side had no traffic at all. We guessed it would beat where we were. So I made a sharp right off Massachusetts Avenue, and we soon found ourselves inextricably headed toward a dark tunnel with tracks between our tires. We realized we had turned onto a trolley way and were about to go underground. If we tried to make a U-turn, an oncoming trolley might arrive and clobber us. Panic! I figured, however, that we'd be safe going in because there were tracks coming out as well as going in, and at least we were on the right side. The tunnel had to exit somewhere, I thought. In we went. I turned on the car lights. After a long downhill curve to our right, we arrived at the Harvard Square platform. The station strained with commuters, but instead of a trolley, they saw us arrive down below the platform. I rolled down my window to look up past their shoelaces and asked, "Is there a way out of here?" More flabbergasted than we were, they pointed straight ahead. I put the car in gear, then scooted off. We soon exited on Mt. Auburn Street, many blocks from where we wanted to be but still in one piece, untrammeled by a trolley.

At Harvard, we stayed in a dorm (Kirkland House, room D-11). Cupit slept in the same bed as Henry David Thoreau had—or so they said. In my journal, I wrote, "I surely would like to go to law school there." Scott and I won four and lost four, a mediocre record. Joe and Danny did even worse. Individually, however, I ranked in the top ten percent. It was a long trip home—twenty-eight hours of humping it with no rests. We had played too much in New York, and it showed in Cambridge.

We had let MSU down.

We bounced back at our next big tournament, a huge competition in Miami. Scott and I went 6–0. I won two "excellents" for oratory and extemporaneous speaking. Overall, we had a good year.

Publicly, the school administration put out press releases extolling the victories of our debate team. Privately, within some administration circles the members of the debate team were viewed as troublemakers. In May 1966, for example, Junior, who wasn't on the debate team, had been walking past the cafeteria when a bouncer stationed outside the cafeteria hall to keep out blacks and other "unwanted guests" from nearby Starkville, engaged Junior, saying, "Well, they've done it now." Junior stopped and asked who had done what. The bouncer said, "Why, the communists are taking over the state legislature and want to legalize liquor. Pretty soon, they'll be letting communists speak on campus." Junior replied, "Well, at least we won't have to be laughed at by the other fifty states." Referring to a YMCA program, the bouncer answered, "What! Why, there was a fellow talking about premarital sex in a lecture last week." Junior replied that he had enough sense not to be misled by one man's opinion. The bouncer then said, "Wait a minute. I know who you are—*you're on that debate team.*"*

---

* When Danny and I learned that the bouncer was there to keep out blacks, we paid a visit to President Colvard to explain what was going on at the front door of the cafeteria hall. Dr. Colvard reacted with surprise, said he had not known, and would look into it. In a few days, the bouncer left, never to return, one of Dr. Colvard's departing good deeds before he left for North Carolina.

29

Inspired by Bobby

Robert Kennedy also set the stage for our year of tumult. Columnists widely speculated that he would challenge Lyndon Johnson for the Democratic nomination (as he eventually did). RFK became an electrifying draw, much sought after for speeches.

In the spring of 1966, during our junior year, a speaker's bureau at the University of Mississippi invited Kennedy, by then a senator from New York, to address the Ole Miss campus. He agreed to do so. Quite a reversal of events, given that less than four years earlier, RFK as attorney general had forced integration upon Ole Miss, a fatal riot had ensued, and the Jackson papers, true to form, had blamed the Kennedys. On March 18, 1966, Kennedy gave a speech at Ole Miss in its basketball gymnasium before six thousand attendees. The event was besieged by protests, but, at the end, he received a standing ovation. To attend this historic event, Cermette organized a caravan from MSU to the Oxford campus. Cermette and Danny met the senator at a reception. Cermette was so taken by Kennedy's blue pinstripe suit that he went and bought one for himself.

Later the same day—a logistical feat for Kennedy and his team—Joe and I attended a similar Kennedy event at the University of Alabama. With us was Frank Whittington, one of our HH stalwarts from Jackson. Frank had organized our trip. He had wrangled VIP treatment for us, and we, too, got to meet the Senator and Ethel Kennedy at a reception. Like the Ole Miss contingent, we were swept away. Kennedy had but a modest frame and spoke quietly, yet he exuded a powerful charisma. He was tan and athletic—quite possibly, it seemed, someone who really could hike fifty miles in a single day. Ethel, too, it so appeared. They seemed pleased with the fact that so many locals joined them at a fully integrated event, then still an unusual occurrence in Dixie.

Part of his speech, aimed at the students and delivered in that marvelous Kennedy style, was this (italics in the original):

> I take this as an occasion to mean that we can talk, now, not as Southerners and Northerners, but as Americans from different parts of a single nation; as partners in a common future. This is the time—and yours is the generation, North and South, Black and White—that can not only remedy the mistakes which *all* of us have made in the past; you can transcend them.

As at Ole Miss, his speech on civil rights (the same basic speech at both colleges) received a standing ovation at Alabama. On reflection, even today, I think national leaders like Robert Kennedy may not appreciate the powerful influence they and their speeches can have on students in remote, often overlooked places like Mississippi and Alabama. The RFK appearances inspired us and encouraged us in the idea that we too at MSU could, even should, sponsor such well-known speakers to illuminate the divide among us and to help find common ground, a quest that would become the centerpiece of our final year at MSU.

Three days after the Kennedy speech, our progressive crowd, variously drawn from the Y program and the debate team, inspired by RFK, came together to run a slate of officers to shake up the MSU student government. Our first organizing meeting was March 21 in Room 210. Those most heavily involved from the outset were Danny, Cermette, Camilla, Scott, Susan, Frank, Jack, Debbie, Joe, and Walter Dowdle (others omitted only for simplicity). I served as the coordinator. Once we felt we had a viable organization and plan, we turned to Joe as our candidate for student body president. He accepted and thus brought to bear the backing of Kappa Alpha, his fraternity, which included Walter and Sidney. Walter proved to be vigorous in campaigning for Joe and soon became active in the leadership of the YMCA as well.

By tradition, the student body presidency had been swapped back and forth each year via a gentlemen's agreement between two dominant fraternities (Joe's not among them). Between those two, there had been sufficient resources to steamroll any miscellaneous competitors. We intended to change that. To tee up our campaign, we put out a questionnaire to students asking for their views on the important issues. We used the results of eleven hundred responses to refine our platform.

We called our campaign "Mandate for Change" and included the following goals:

> To promote the on-campus right of students to hear
> off-campus speakers.
> To work for more realistic rules for women students.
> To work for better entertainment.
> To promote student evaluations of instructors.

For example, we asked: If it was really true, as the conservative dean of students said, that parents didn't want their daughters wearing shorts and slacks, then why shouldn't they be allowed a parental permission slip to indicate that they could wear shorts and slacks? By 1966, the enrollment of women at MSU had grown rapidly, and women filled three dorms. Our Mandate for Change campaign got kudos from women students. Susan Eiland served as a dorm organizer.*

We stole a march. On the first night that campaigning was allowed, our precinct workers, all previously organized, fanned out in the dorms to hand out our literature and to ask students to tune in to our radio broadcast that very night. At ten o'clock, Scott Wendelsdorf went live on the local radio station, WSSO. Fifteen of us (women, too) crowded into Room 210 to listen—as did thousands of other students across the campus. Scott's voice came on the air, reading from his own handwritten script (which I still have):

> Students of Mississippi State University, the time for change is at

---

* Dwight Eisenhower had titled the first volume of his presidential memoir *Mandate For Change*—but we didn't realize that and only coincidentally landed on the same name.

hand! For the first time in the University's history, you the students are presented with the opportunity to achieve the goals—the freedoms—the privileges you have been striving for.

Just a few hours ago, the Student Administration Senate approved the candidacy of a slate of proposed officers who run united—not as individuals with limited influence—but as a united front standing on a common platform—standing with a common goal. The platform is one of significant change—not meek echo. The goal is one of achievement to secure those changes wanted and demanded by you, the students—not a solidification of the status quo.

Scott had the perfect voice for this, crisp and brisk, his mid-tones predominating with a Midwest accent. Each word was enunciated. His pauses proved perfect. It was the same clear directness that helped us win debates. But more, his voice carried the electricity of a signal moment on campus. Continuing, he told how the campaign originated:

Over a month ago, this movement to secure student demands was born. A group of interested and concerned students came together to form a central committee. We were interested in the needs and desires of you, the students, and we were concerned also—concerned because past student elections, student administration officials, and administration edicts have done little to achieve the goals which the students seek.

Scott then described the committee's student survey:

To determine exactly what changes were wanted by the students and if in fact these changes would be feasible ones, we undertook the most extensive student survey in MSU history. On March 23, 1100 of you, representing a cross-section of the student body, were polled to determine what issues concerned you and what changes you wanted to see. In other words, we went to the people to find the true feelings on the issues. Our resulting platform is not a product of the smoke-filled caucus room—it is a platform suggested and formulated by you, the student body.

After describing other work of the committee, Scott captured our message in two sentences:

> You the students of MSU issued a mandate for change. And we have accepted it.

His radio broadcast then summarized our platform. Finally, Scott ended as follows:

> We've made our stand. We are committed. If you really care what happens to State, if you want change, then join us—stand with us and be counted.

Scott's speech thrilled the campus. In the past, student campaigns had been desultory, having been rigged Mississippi-style. Now, "mandate for change" became the number one phrase on campus. We caught the other two candidates by total surprise. There was one glitch, however. As I confided to my journal, "Only one thing—Scott referred to us twice as the 'Central Committee.' Some people began to wonder if this meant 'the Party.'"

Joe challenged the other two candidates to a debate. They declined on the ground that Joe was a "professional debater." Joe replied, "The meat is afraid to come to the grinder," a line he borrowed from Robert Kennedy.

We had radio ads. We had literature. We had banners, bumper stickers, and handbills promoting Mandate for Change, and a flyer detailing our platform was distributed by the hundreds. We gave talks in the dorms. We raised money. As just one example of our fundraising efforts, several of us went through the dorms collecting "Pennies For Progress" and raised a couple of hundred dollars. Joe's frat brothers dug deeper to support the cause. We had a well-oiled dorm-by-dorm, even floor-by-floor, grassroots organization to spread the message.

The night before the vote there was a big outdoor assembly on the steps of the new Colvard Student Union. Although there was no debate format, all three candidates spoke, using the public-address system. Bright lights flooded the lectern. Joe excelled, hammering home issue after issue. A thousand students jammed in to watch. Enthusiasm soared. Our essential message rang out—that it was time for change, time to bring MSU into the twentieth century. Cheering, laughter, and applause echoed off the walls.

But in the shadowy recesses of the administration offices in nearby Lee Hall, where the status quo loomed ever large, anxiety mounted.

In the first vote, Joe won a plurality. The status quo opponent—the traditional frat candidate—came in *last*. Hallelujah! Specifically, Joe got 1,050 votes and the other two candidates got 930 and 900, respectively. We'd beaten the system. So, we'd won that round in more ways than one.

For the runoff, however, the odds leaned against us, for we could not expect the Old Guard votes to go to Joe. Worse, we did not work for Joe as hard as we should have in the runoff. We rested too much on our laurels from the first vote. A bad omen—our campaign's upright piano bounced out of a pickup truck as it rolled up University Drive and busted up right in front of Lee Hall. In the final vote, the compromise candidate won.

Still, we celebrated. We'd stirred things up and placed our issues on page one. At least we'd helped elect a more moderate slate. The compromise candidate, in fact, also resided in the student YMCA and would prove to be a most decent alternative.

I WON THE ELECTION for president of the student YMCA for the upcoming school year. On May 13, 1966, in the YMCA auditorium, I assumed the office at an annual banquet. My mom came, her only visit to MSU. She beamed with pride in her quiet way. It was her gentle face—slightly more radiant than usual. I gave a short speech. Camilla said to my mom, "I don't believe I have been so stirred by a speech since the 1961 inauguration." Bless her. Even my dad would have been proud, especially knowing that his son verged on the college degree he would have cherished.

A BRUTAL BEATING OCCURRED right in front of the YMCA as the school year came to a close. The beating seemed aimed at progressive ideas. In May 1966, the Encampment for Citizenship, a foundation supported by Eleanor Roosevelt until her death in 1962, asked to use our YMCA conference room to conduct interviews for summer intern positions. The liberal group sponsored a summer camp to promote democratic ideals. We, of course, extended the courtesy. John Davis, a liberal faculty member in the anthropology department, greeted the foundation representative, Douglas Kelley, a recent Peace Corps volunteer. After the interviews, just as Kelley exited the YMCA, two roughs approached. They smashed Kelley over the head with a thick glass Coke bottle, using it like a billy club, then snatched his briefcase. Kelley fell to the ground, bleeding and losing consciousness. He survived. The two thugs escaped (with the briefcase). The police never solved the crime. Was it safe, some of us asked, to call for progressive reform?

30

The Meredith March and Dr. King

For Danny and me, in different ways, the summer of 1966 became a sustained, important season to learn from the civil rights movement. The summer began for both of us with a civil rights rally at Tougaloo College. For me, the summer ended in a Chicago church listening to Dr. Martin Luther King Jr., and for Danny, it ended in Jackson in a one-on-one talk with Dr. King in his hotel room. Like the summer before, I lived in the Y and took classes so I could graduate on time despite changing my major from engineering to math. Danny worked for the statewide Young Democrats. I didn't get assigned a summer roommate, so I had Room 210 to myself.

The March Against Fear, one of the most famous of the civil rights marches—and the most famous of the Mississippi marches—began with one man. On June 6, 1966, James Meredith (by then an Ole Miss graduate), began a solitary walk from Memphis to Jackson—220 miles—as a protest against racism. On his second day of walking, he was gunned down along the side of the road (but survived, thankfully, and was able to rejoin the march by the end). Dr. King, Stokely Carmichael, and many others caught the fallen banner and pressed on with the Meredith march. When they reached Greenwood, about halfway to Jackson, Carmichael delivered his famous "Black Power" speech, and the new slogan immediately began to compete with the "Freedom Now" slogan of Dr. King's Southern Christian Leadership Conference. In Canton, closer to Jackson, the marchers were tear-gassed by state police; no one was killed but several were brutally injured. The penultimate stop was a large rally at Tougaloo College, a few miles north of Jackson. James Brown, Sammy Davis Jr., and Dick Gregory entertained.

The march ended the next day in Jackson with a rally on the capitol steps.

I observed the march twice, attended the Tougaloo rally, then circulated my observations in the HH newsletter a few days later. Near noon on Friday, June 24, I drove alone in my new VW bug through Canton, about thirty minutes north of Jackson, on my normal route home from MSU. As I reached Canton's town center, a tense calm prevailed. Clots of highway patrolmen, game and fish wardens, and local police, all white, stood at the ready in shady spots near the town square. Newsmen and cameramen spread out in force, too, also all white. The marchers, numbering several hundred, mostly blacks with some whites, walked on the left side of the road. The newsmen stuck to the right, wearing white short-sleeved shirts. As I slowed with the heavy traffic to cross a cluster of train tracks, a young white guy with long wavy hair and a walkie-talkie shouted, "Come on, everyone is invited." Smiling, three young black women then scurried between the cars to join the marchers. Though sweating and road-weary, the marchers seemed in a festive mood, singing, "We're marching on down (clap), marching on to freedom (clap) . . ." They carried handmade placards. Airplanes circled, and a helicopter hovered.

Not long after I drove through, the festive mood turned ugly. The state police used tear gas and batons, the media later reported, to break up and arrest many of the marchers right near where I'd been.

The next afternoon, Danny and I drove north from Jackson on Interstate 55, then began our return via old Highway 51, the march route that day to Tougaloo College. We wanted to see its full length for ourselves. We were planning to join the rally at Tougaloo that night. The radio interrupted frequently to inform listeners of the exact location of the marchers. Out-of-state plates were everywhere—likewise the state troopers. Planes and a helicopter circled above. Spectators of both races lined the sides of the old highway, remaining even after the marchers had passed. We saw march stragglers. We saw newsmen running about with film canisters. Carloads of supporters "riding for freedom" whizzed by. We could tell where the main body of the march lay just by watching the helicopter.

We eventually reached the support vehicles, including a supply truck followed by a slow-moving ambulance at the ready. Then, the actual marchers came into view, their number now reduced to about one hundred. No was singing. One sign read, "Move on over or we'll move on over you." One man wore a doctor's lab coat. A nurse walked with him. A tall white priest dressed all in black must have been very hot. No famous face appeared as we passed. Ahead of the lead marchers rolled a flatbed truck with film crews facing rearward, cameras whirring away.

The marchers looked determined; they did not show the carefree spirit of the day before. Since then, they'd been tear-gassed by state police. You had to admire anyone who could march even a part of that 220-mile trek from Memphis to Jackson, especially in the oven of summer—but especially in the teeth of such danger. I was surprised by the number of young white women marching, in sweaty, road-worn clothes. One was movie-star beautiful and might have been from Hollywood. Young white guys with Dylan hair marched too. One old white lady had a wet towel wrapped about her head. It was Mississippi hot and might turn Mississippi mean at any moment.

That evening, Danny and I attended the rally at Tougaloo College, our first real civil rights rally. Danny had a paying summer job organizing for the Mississippi Young Democrats and wanted to go to the rally to show support. He asked me to go with him. We hoped Dr. King would appear on stage to exhort the troops. We wanted to see and hear him in the flesh. We wanted to support the cause.

The Sovereignty Commission snoops no doubt lurked, so Danny's license plate number surely got noted that night. We parked in an open grass field with hundreds of other vehicles, then walked to the rally. The event was already underway; we saw the bright lights of the stage ahead through the dark trees and took in the warm, deep aroma of a summer night in Mississippi. Hundreds of blacks, many with dates, gathered on grassy slopes on the outer reaches of the audience. A few whites mixed in, too. Fireflies blinked. As we approached, the announcer on a loudspeaker said, "The difference between a Freedom Rally and a Klan cross burning is that a Klan rally don't have top Hollywood entertainers." At the gate, "Freedom Now" buttons and bumper stickers were on sale.

Danny and I found a spot near a platform for film cameras. We had a good view. On the stage, Dick Gregory, asked for donations, saying, "This rally and march has cost us $34,000 . . . so we don't want contributions tonight, we want sacrifices." Then he told a story about the difference between a contribution versus a sacrifice, which involved "the difference between what a hen versus a hog provide for breakfast." James Meredith and Stokely Carmichael spoke. The Freedom Singers ended the entertainment with an a cappella rendition of "Pick a Bale of Cotton." Instructions for the Sunday march into Jackson then followed. To our disappointment, Dr. King gave no speech (though he stood in the crowd on the stage for a while). The rally over, the massive, upbeat crowd flowed slowly out of the gates. At our exit, a man holding a collection box chanted, "Dig deep . . . Yes, sir . . . Black Power . . . Thank you . . . Yes ma'am . . . Black Power . . . Those dollars mean Black Power . . . Thank you," and so on.

Danny noticed the box of cash and said to him, "You mean green power, don't you?"

The man replied, "Yes, sir, that's what I said, Black Power."

Black Power was the trademark of the hour.

The Tougaloo rally for the March Against Fear was a first for Danny and me. Yes, we figured that the Sovereignty Commission had our tag number, but we wanted to join in. We were proud that we did.

Danny came back to the Y for a couple of days—but not for school. His summer job organizing for the Mississippi Young Democrats was the start of Danny's long and rich contribution to the Democratic party, a relationship in which he has asked for little but given much. Danny got involved with the Young Democrats through Flavous Hutchinson, the professor we had promoted for a judgeship to Charles Evers. On campus, Joe Turnage was our MSU YD vice president. Frank Whittington was our treasurer, and I was our secretary. Truth be told, our little campus group of Young Democrats amounted only to the Higgen Hogs.

In the 1960s, the regular Democratic Party in Mississippi continued as a fossil of the Old South, represented by, for example, Senator James Eastland, one of the most racist figures in American history. At that time in Mississippi, the Republican Party was the progressive party, but it could not muster the votes needed to win any statewide office. To bring the

Mississippi Democrats more in line with the national party (and to provide a more moderate alternative to the Mississippi Freedom Democratic Party), the Mississippi Young Democrats stepped forward. Hodding Carter III and Cleveland Donald became co-chairs. Hodding Carter III was the managing editor and associate publisher of the *Delta Democrat-Times*, the newspaper in Greenville that his father had famously founded and run, sometimes then called the "Conscience of the Delta." Cleveland Donald was the second black graduate of Ole Miss.

That summer, Danny and Cleveland Donald organized local Young Democrat clubs around the state. On Wednesday, June 29, 1966, they stayed in the Y dorm, Danny with me in Room 210 and Cleveland with Coleman Chong, our suitemate. Cleveland was the first black to sleep in an MSU dorm, even if for only one night, with the possible exception of Richard Holmes, who eventually took up residence in a dorm after first commuting from home in Starkville. In those days, despite passage of the Civil Rights Act two years earlier, it remained hard for any black visitor to find a public accommodation in Mississippi.

Later in the summer, I interviewed Danny for the HH newsletter. Here is a part of that feature from the newsletter ("NL" stands for newsletter):

> On an Indian summer evening, we called on [Cupit] in his Suite in the YMCA—commonly known as the "hotbed for liberals." He was very cordial and glad to give the NEWSLETTER an interview. He was dressed in socks, underpants and a Penny's T-shirt. He sat on his bed that was not made up—and somehow one got the feeling that he was in a muggy room with a typewriter and a mimeograph. On his bookshelf we noted several copies of *The Closed Society, Kennedy, The Cause Is Mankind*, etc. We turned on the tape recorder and the questioning was easy. . . .
>
> *NL:* Exactly what was your job this summer?
>
> *Cupit:* Well, Bill, I was an organizer for the Young Democratic Clubs of Mississippi, which is the only officially recognized Democratic party in this State. As a result of contributions from various sources, we were able to put on salary three people including two full time organizers—who traveled about setting up chapters.

NL: Was this on a bi-racial concept?

Cupit: Yes it was. This is the only bi-racial political party in this State. Incidentally, Bill, one of our organizers was a Negro, Cleveland Donald, a graduate of the University of Mississippi. I was the other.

NL: What one person has most voiced opposition to the YD's in Mississippi?

Cupit: Any long-time politician in this State would be opposed to it because we are threatening the stranglehold they have on our citizens. The most outspoken would have to be Tom Ethridge, who in his bigoted, racist column, has made several blasting and chiding comments about our organization. He has dealt mainly in half-truths and untruths about us and our leaders.

NL: Would you connect RFK's support of the YD's here in Mississippi to his plans to run for the Presidency in 1972?

Cupit: Of course, I can't speak for the Senator. But anyone seeking the Presidency is going to make sure the votes are going his way. In 1972, under the age of 30 will comprise about one-third of the population. Those in college now will be politically influential by 1972. Robert Kennedy, in closing, gives my views concerning the YD's. He said, "Each of us will ultimately be judged on the extent to which he has personally contributed to the life of his nation and the world society which we are trying to build. Only as countrymen and brothers can we pursue our personal talents to the limits of our possibility—not as Southerners, black or white, or Northerners—but as men and women in the service of the American dream." He said that at Ole Miss last March 18.

Bill Silver, son of famed Ole Miss professor James Silver, author of *Mississippi: The Closed Society*, served as the executive secretary of the Young Democrats in Mississippi. Bill asked me to run the "program" for a meeting in the African American community for the Oktibbeha County YD effort. (MSU and Starkville fell in Oktibbeha County.) I was green as hell and worried that I would unintentionally insult someone. And I worried that the whole enterprise would be under surveillance by white supremacists. Nevertheless, one evening I went door-to-door, alone, in Starkville's black neighborhood talking up the upcoming event. I sensed polite suspicion from those who answered my knock. For all they knew, I could have been a Klan member posing as a voting-rights advocate.

On Tuesday, July 5, I was pleasantly surprised. Fourteen blacks and three whites turned out for the meeting at a funeral home. I explained the Young Democrats, then asked those seventeen to help form the local club. I explained that our YD goals were to (1) register white and black voters, (2) infiltrate local precinct meetings of regular Democratic parties to elect moderate or liberal delegates to the 1968 statewide convention and thus to keep in good standing with the national party, and (3) run candidates for local office where the incumbents were ultra right-wingers or bigots, which included Oktibbeha County. The group responded well, even applied for a charter. A local physician, Dr. Douglas Conner (Richard Holmes's stepfather), attended and volunteered to follow up on voter registration. This was a first for me—my first (and only) direct action to address the exclusion of blacks from the ballot box. I had just turned twenty-one.

A month later, my journal for August 3, 1966, stated:

> Pleased to learn that last week 30 people requested to vote as a result of the Young Democrats club in Okt. County.

The voter effort moved into the more capable hands of Dr. Conner, and I receded when the school year began. Nevertheless, my small effort represented a tiny personal step along the road to true democracy. And, thankfully, no violence ever attended any of these efforts.

THAT SUMMER, I HAD the remarkable good fortune to see and hear Dr. Martin Luther King Jr. in the pulpit. As the incoming president of the campus YMCA, an opportunity arose near summer's end for me to attend a workshop in Chicago on urban poverty. The workshop was sponsored by the National Student Council of YMCAs. During the 1950s, the National Council of YMCAs had taken a position favoring integration. In response, the MSU administration at the time demanded that the MSU YMCA cease its affiliation with the National Council. In our era, we therefore remained independent of the national organization, but Cermette arranged for me to attend as a Southern Area delegate anyway. This led to my first flight on a commercial plane and a week-plus trip in late August 1966.

The conference lasted from Sunday, August 28, to Thursday, September 1, 1966, and was held at the Illinois Institute of Technology in Chicago. The conference was run by theology students involved with the Chicago Freedom Movement, a summer-long protest led by Dr. Martin Luther King and the SCLC over segregated, terrible living conditions for African Americans in Chicago. My first impression of the student conference was off-putting. The opening "prayer" reeked with profanity—in poor taste, I thought to myself, not my brand of Christianity. I lightened up, however, as the conference proceeded.

On our first full day, we "plunged" into the city slums in small groups of four or five, each led by one of the theology students. "Plunge" became the conference theme. And plunge we did. In our first day, I saw more poverty than anyone could ever want to see. In those ragged and filthy grass-free blocks, we felt broken glass beneath our shoes and smelled rotting buildings, many built as temporary housing after the Chicago Fire in 1871, all rat-infested, yet all still occupied. One school suffered under a thunderous elevated train track. No child could have heard herself think there, much less learn. Due to race discrimination in employment, African Americans lost out on good jobs, so they lacked funds to live anywhere outside of the ghetto even if discriminatory housing policies had been reformed; it was a vicious cycle. Before I went to this conference, I had thought the average black did not care much about the issue of urban poverty. Mayor Richard Daley had famously said in 1963, "There are no ghettos in Chicago," and I had given him the benefit of the doubt, but now our eyes and noses told us otherwise. He was so wrong. I came away convinced that the entire black community cared deeply about the problem and that widespread discrimination against individuals accumulated to a systemic evil on a large scale.

Near the end of the conference, one of the conference organizers, a student at the Chicago Theological Seminary, invited me and my conference roommate to join him at a mass meeting after dinner in support of the Chicago Freedom Project. The main event was to be Dr. Martin Luther

King Jr., who had been dividing his time between the Meredith March and Chicago but was now back in Chicago full-time. This was not an official conference activity, but a proposed adventure of our own. We accepted the invitation. Junior's father had put it this way: "That man can make a speech." I wanted to hear him give one.

No one since has had the presence Dr. King had in those days. By 1966, he already loomed larger than life. Ten years earlier, he had led the Montgomery Bus Boycott ignited by Mrs. Rosa Parks. He co-founded and led the Southern Christian Leadership Conference, battled vicious discrimination in Birmingham, electrified the March on Washington with his "I Have A Dream" oration, walked at the head of the Selma to Montgomery March, and unapologetically insisted that the Kennedy and Johnson administrations push hard for civil rights legislation. He had won the Nobel Peace Prize in 1964. All over the South, however, were billboards showing a photograph of Dr. King supposedly attending a communist training camp. Hated, loved, feared, admired, ridiculed, and praised, Dr. King was then the subject of passionately divided opinion.

His battlegrounds had all been in the South. Now, however, Dr. King and the SCLC had joined a new front, an assault on a Northern ghetto and its root causes—job and housing discrimination. Earlier that summer, he had led a march from Soldier Field to City Hall to affix a copy of the movement's demands to the front door. Heckled and harassed, he strode out front into white neighborhoods like Gage Park, then to the doorsteps of realtors who openly practiced race discrimination. After a march through an all-white neighborhood on August 5 when King was stoned by thugs, he said that he had not seen such hostility and hate even in Mississippi and Alabama.

In only the thirty-six months preceding the summer of 1966, assassins and mobs had killed, among many others, Medgar Evers, Michael Schwerner, James Chaney, Andrew Goodman, Viola Liuzzo, four young girls at Birmingham's Sixteenth Street Baptist Church, and, of course, President Kennedy. Dr. King himself had been the intended target of bombings in Alabama and stone-throwing in Chicago. He had been jailed, tear-gassed, smeared as a communist, and hounded by the FBI. He had stood up to Bull Connor in Birmingham, Sheriff Clark in Selma, and Mayor Daley in Chicago. Surrounded by a smoldering white mob that very summer in Philadelphia, Mississippi, he had confronted Deputy Sheriff Cecil Ray Price, face-to-face, with: "You're the one who had Schwerner and those fellows in jail." He had then pointedly told the mob: "I believe in my heart that the murderers are somewhere around me at this moment." He was right. Dr. King's own life remained constantly in danger.

After dinner on Wednesday, August 31, 1966, the three of us went down to the South Side on the elevated train. As we exited, we got caught up in the gathering flood of spirited attendees moving toward the Liberty Baptist Church, where a large, high-ceilinged sanctuary brimmed almost full an hour before the meeting's scheduled start. We sat two-thirds of the way back, three white faces in a sea of dark ones, about two thousand altogether. As the time drew near, more and more humanity pressed into the pews until all were jammed hard against one another. Many stood.

The evening light of midsummer had faded from the large sanctuary windows when, well after the appointed hour, after others had rallied the room, a slight commotion stirred among the entourage near the pastor's entrance. Then, without formality of introduction, there before us stood Dr. Martin Luther King Jr. Physically, Dr. King stood shorter than I had expected. He had broad shoulders and seemed most solid. He wore a dark suit and white shirt and tie. His face showed weariness and determination. There were no broad smiles or celebratory handshakes. Once he appeared, the mood went from jubilance to reverence. The assemblage hushed.

Dr. King began speaking softly and slowly, matter-of-factly, as if finding his meter. The weariness in his voice seemed, at first, to match his face. He had come from a meeting with Major Richard Daley, he said, the reason for his lateness. He spoke calmly of the day's negotiations, its details, the very news the hall wished to hear.

Soon, however, chants of "Black Power" drowned him out. Dr. King asked if someone wanted to speak. A SNCC leader, Albert Monroe Sharp, stepped forward and addressed the meeting. His main point was opposition to even negotiating with the white power structure. A few days later, I summarized his speech in an HH newsletter:

When I was at the rally, Monroe Sharp and his SNCC crew chanted Black Power until King let him speak. He explained black power as simply black people realizing that they were people and that they could be successful if they tried. They had to be proud—not ashamed—of being black. They had to shun the white man's welfare that kept him in poverty and build economic strength of their own.

When Dr. King resumed, he disagreed with Sharp and remarked that whenever the Pharaoh wanted to keep the slaves in bondage, he kept them fighting among themselves, a remark that was more warmly received than Sharp's interruption (which had received only polite applause). Dr. King suggested a "dress-in" at a well-known department store in Chicago that wouldn't negotiate with their union. He announced that another march would be necessary (scheduled to leave from that very church). Finally, Dr. King moved on to the familiar themes of the movement. His voice found a pulpit cadence. He stressed the need for nonviolence, described the fallacy of violence, and reiterated the irresistibility of peaceful protest. History is on our side. Justice is on our side. God is on our side. Keep the faith. Keep the peace. He used only plain speech and the human voice, both whisper and anthem, but they came from his heart and moved us. I was moved.

While I got to hear and see Dr. King give one of his pulpit exhortations, Danny actually met the great man and had a one-on-one talk. Earlier that summer, the SCLC held a celebratory dinner in Jackson where Senator Ted Kennedy gave a speech. Beforehand, Danny (as part of his Young Democrats job) attended a planning and strategy group meeting where he met Dr. King. The next day, on his own initiative, Danny went to Dr. King's hotel room, talked with him, and asked Dr. King to inscribe a copy of his book *Strength to Love*. He did. Danny still has the inscribed copy.

I believe, as do many others, that Dr. King was the greatest orator of our age. Was he also the greatest American of our time? I think so. He completely gave himself to a peaceful, just, and paramount cause, knowing that he would likely be called to give his life as well. And, in 1968, he did give his life, but his cause carried on to make America a better nation. What Gandhi did for India, Dr. King did for America.

FROM AN EARLY AGE, I believed that every citizen in a democracy should be allowed to vote. Democracy had triumphed over tyranny in the Second World War, a victory that suffused Americans with pride in those years. To my young mind, it bears repeating, the essence of democracy meant that everyone, including blacks, should vote. But as I mentioned earlier, just as everyone should be free to vote for anyone they wished, my original thought was that landlords, proprietors, and employers should be free to deal or not deal with anyone they pleased. It was a free country, I thought. Let decency win out on its own. Let each follow his or her own conscience. The Civil Rights Act of 1964, however, answered that moral question as a matter of law as to employment and public accommodations.

I saw why in Chicago. When it came to the basics of life—employment, education, and housing—individual discrimination based on race added up to systemic blights like we'd seen in Chicago. The sum of all private and individual discrimination produced massive denials of opportunity based on nothing other than skin color. One of the strengths of our nation continued to be the willingness of Americans to put in a hard day's work—and after Chicago, I fervently believed that opportunity for employment, along with housing and everything else should, by law, be equal for all without regard to race. That experience in Chicago—seeing the inhuman slums, seeing the systemic discrimination, hearing Albert Monroe Sharp and Dr. King—thoroughly convinced me that race discrimination should be outlawed in all its forms and should not be left to individual choice. (Shortly after Dr. King's assassination in 1968, Congress enacted the Fair Housing Act, which outlawed discrimination in the sale, rental, and financing of housing.)

In my journal, I grappled with this new understanding:

> The problem is vast there and I could not help but relate it to home. Here, we don't have ghettoes but we have discrimination—and like everywhere—we have prejudice. And prejudice has existed for hundreds of years. And how foolish it is to think that we in this generation will see the end of even a majority of it. It is vast and will take years of mind-changing to allow the Negro to be color-blind and to allow the white to be color-blind.

We knew that Mississippi had terrible poverty of its own, though we had never "plunged" into it. In Mississippi, I had thought the main problem was denial of voting rights, and I had imagined that solving that problem would lead to solutions on all the other race-related problems, given the large black population in Mississippi. Yet, in Chicago, African Americans had the franchise, but the ghetto had nonetheless persisted. Eliminating race discrimination in voting would not be enough. The problems remained worse, more complex. Race discrimination on a broader scale had to end. It took a plunge into the worst Chicago had to offer for me to see the problem and, in turn, to see the problem as it really existed right under my own nose in Mississippi.

As a boy, I had frowned on marches, sit-ins, and demonstrations, thinking that they led to violence (which they often had). Like many white moderates in America at the time, I had preferred genteel dialogue to direct action. But the Meredith March, the Chicago Campaign, and the March on Washington showed me that peaceful protest ranked as a revered right—one essential to making democracy work. By the end of the summer of 1966, I had come to a profound new understanding. A *peaceful* assembly to petition the government for redress of grievance was crucial, I came to see, to draw attention to an evil and to promote a remedy. That, too, was indispensable to democracy. If *onlookers* became violent and threw stones, *they* should be locked up, *not* the peaceful protesters. Later in law school and while clerking with Justice William O. Douglas, I learned the law and theory behind equal protection of the law, freedom of peaceful assembly, and petition for redress. But before I had ever cracked a law book, the summer of 1966 taught me a visceral faith in these principles, as essential to a true democracy as the right to vote.

31

Katrina

It's August 27, 2005. The phone ruins a perfectly good Saturday afternoon nap in Oakland.

"Alsup, this is Cupit. Listen, what are Allison and Gavin doing about the hurricane?"

"What hurricane?"

"The big hurricane about to hit New Orleans, head-on. They've got a mandatory evacuation order. Why don't they come here to Jackson and ride it out with us?"

"The last one," I reply, "they rode out in New Orleans." Our daughter and son-in-law have lived in New Orleans for five years.

"Yeah, but this one's bigger. Everyone's gotta leave."

"My God, okay. Thanks. I'll call 'em now."

Repeatedly, I try Allison, but the trunk lines for New Orleans are overwhelmed. Late that night, I finally get through.

I relay Cupit's offer, worried that they may want to stay put.

"Yeah, Dad, we're leaving in the morning. Gavin's packing now. We've decided we've got to go this time. This one's too big and too close."

Allison seems relieved, grateful to have a place to land. They already know Danny and his wife, Sharon, having attended various *HH* reunions. I give her their number.

"I'll call right now," she says.

The exodus before Katrina will rank among the worst refugee dramas in American history—bumper to bumper, totally gridlocked traffic, paralysis on the freeway across Lake Ponchatrain (and all other routes out of New

Orleans). After many tense hours, Allison and Gavin and their three animals make the far shore of the lake, still very much in harm's way, then abandon the freeway in favor of back roads, trusting to luck, heading north. Lashed by the leading band of the hurricane at a dusk rest break near Hazelhurst, they rescue a kitten, shivering and soaked under a bush. Now with four animals, they meander north in the storm and make Danny's by midnight. They stay a week with Danny and Sharon, helping remove a storm-downed tree blown against their house. Then they go on to Houston and take advantage of an apartment generously offered through an Oakland neighbor. Sidney and Walter, who live in Houston, help them move in and supply them with all essentials. A month passes before New Orleans officials allow residents back in. Gavin drives there to see what's left.

Their house survived, unflooded, a miracle.

32

A Stand Against Evil

When we reunited in Room 210 in September 1966, Danny and I rode the catbird seats. He came fresh off his Young Democrats summer with plans to make a political splash on campus, and I was fresh off my own memorable summer, ready to lead the YMCA. Within a few weeks, however, we would find ourselves at the center of a politically charged fight over the statewide ban against any "controversial" speaker coming onto a college campus. The specific issue at hand—whether we would be allowed to bring a black speaker to campus. In 1966, no black speaker had ever addressed an audience at a white college in Mississippi.

We had a top-drawer team in place on the Y cabinet. Walter Dowdle served as vice president, Debbie Davis as secretary, and Garland Robertson (our suitemate) as treasurer. Scott Wendelsdorf, our debating colleague and "Mandate for Change" radio announcer, became chair of the Student-Faculty Committee. Illustrative of how sixties we were, we even had a "Concern Committee," co-chaired by Peggy Powell and Sam Love, to identify "concerns" of the "community" and the campus and to recommend ways to address them. Our YMCA Concern Committee published a pro and con commentary on political issues (like the speaker ban) called "Synthesis." Cermette, of course, continued as the faculty Director of the YMCA—with great influence. We also had an eleven-member faculty advisory board. Two of our cabinet team, Peggy and Sam, were columnists on the school newspaper, *The Reflector*, so the paper developed a friendly attitude towards our efforts in its editorials.

Frank Whittington served as chair of the "Current Issues" Committee.

He had wrangled our VIP invite to the Kennedy speech (and was a Higgen Hog classmate from Provine). He led our plan to bring in speakers at the forefront of the issue of race in America. Frank also lived in the Y dorm.

We circulated a brochure entitled "Action '67," which described itself as "a brief outline of Y-sponsored programs of action for those students wanting to be involved in the campus and community environment," using three buzz words much in vogue back then—"action," "involved," and "community." Inside the eleven-page, four-by-nine brochure was a description of our mission: "The YMCA enthusiastically provides the battlefield where man's responsibility for and commitment to the world are critically examined and evaluated." Continuing, it proclaimed "that we all must be involved in life and committed to truth and that this involvement and this commitment must be now, not later." More buzzwords—"committed" and "commitment"—other favorites of the 1960s.

Outside the campus, Mississippi continued to be a killing ground for civil rights leaders. Vernon Dahmer, a respected and successful African American businessman in Hattiesburg, Mississippi, stood as a strong advocate of equal voting rights. In January 1966, he made a public offer to collect his neighbors' poll taxes to save them a trip to the courthouse and even volunteered to pay the poll taxes of anyone who couldn't afford them. That night, his home in Hattiesburg was firebombed and shot up by Klan nightriders. In the darkness, he returned the gunfire while his family escaped. He died a few days later from fire injury to his lungs. Both white and black residents of the Hattiesburg community responded with outrage and an outpouring of support for Dahmer's family. Local prosecutors obtained guilty verdicts on three of the Klansmen (and they received life prison terms), but most of the accused escaped justice. Those were the first verdicts in Mississippi to convict whites for a civil rights murder of a black person.

THE CHICAGO CONFERENCE THAT year had been so good that we managed at the end of 1966 (over our Christmas break) to attend another conference in Chicago, also sponsored by the National Student Association of YMCAs. This time four of us went, and the Y paid part of our expenses. Scott, Debbie Davis, Margaret Weeks, and I drove up and back in my VW bug. We were lucky to live through it, for in Arkansas we hit a patch of ice and spun around like a top, coming to rest in a mantle of snow in the median. We pushed the car back onto the road and carried on—but slower.

At the conference, I was taken with the Reverend James Bevel, "MLK's right hand man in Chicago," as I described him in my journal. He had been one of the original Freedom Riders imprisoned in Jackson. Roy Wilkins, executive director of the NAACP, also spoke to us. Hundreds of us, of all races, joined arms in singing "We Shall Overcome" at the grand finale meeting on New Year's Eve.

On a more social note, my journal entry read: "Wendelsdorf and Maggie are pretty thick now. Both of them are radical and are 'made' for each other. This trip cinched it." (In fact, Scott and Margaret would marry right after college.) They were radical, responsibly so, but radical. Maybe Scott had slipped the phrase "central committee" into that radio speech on purpose.

Tom Ethridge and the *Clarion-Ledger*, on January 11, 1967, devoted a column to criticizing "a recent YMCA-YWCA-sponsored college youth conference in Chicago," the very one we had just attended. Ethridge added:

> Advocates of socialism have always realized the importance of captur-
> ing the impressionable minds of youth, and they overlook no effort to
> gain control of the educational process.
>
> SELFISH MOTIVES for promoting socialism and all-powerful gov-
> ernment are apparent, because big government can take from those who
> have and give to those who need—including teachers and professors who
> constantly clamor for more money and never seem satisfied with their pay.

It was the same old propaganda—anyone who imagined a different way of life had to be a communist or socialist. Unfortunately, the regular readers of the *Clarion-Ledger* trusted the paper and its opinions.

But our story has jumped slightly ahead, and we need to go back a few months to the beginning of the academic year in the fall of 1966, that charming moment of college life when all is a blank slate, faces are fresh, and fall crispness accents the fading heat of summer.

THE EVENT THAT WOULD define our time at MSU was the Mississippi "speaker ban" controversy and, in particular, our invitation to Aaron Henry, the black president of the Mississippi NAACP, to speak on campus. Front and center stood the First Amendment, academic freedom, equality, and the search for truth.

Talking it through in our YMCA board room, the corner meeting room off the main lobby, with autumn colors blazing outside the windows, we felt we could promote progress in Mississippi by holding a series of lectures and dialogues featuring outside speakers. We felt we were living through a historic whirlwind of events. We were moved by those events and genuinely wanted to hear what various leaders had to say on the key questions of the time. This format had precedent, even in Mississippi. A lyceum series in the 1920s had brought progressive Wisconsin Senator Robert M. LaFollette to speak on campus. But the format had fallen into disuse. In the tumult of the sixties, we wanted to revive the ancient but powerful lyceum concept.

One of the main ways the white power structure maintained the status quo was by suppressing criticism. Suppression occurred via political correctness—the "correct" viewpoint demanding allegiance to the Mississippi way of life. Suppression also occurred through a speaker ban limiting free speech on all college campuses in the state. Specifically, no one could come onto a college campus in Mississippi to give a speech without the prior approval of the college president, according to a Mississippi regulation.

The regulation arose as a direct response to the Supreme Court's desegregation decision. Beginning in 1955, to suppress "dangerous speakers," the Board of Trustees of the Mississippi State Institutions of Higher Learning had charged university and college presidents with the duty to pre-screen campus speakers. The college board proved extremely conservative and insisted that university and college chiefs prohibit any "invasion" by outside influences with ideas contrary to the established policy of the State of Mississippi. Ole Miss, for example, turned down a proposed speaker who had contributed money to the NAACP and whose wife had written an article in the *Saturday Evening Post* about her experiences teaching African American students. This rejection drew a protest by the American Association of

University Professors, but in our state, such criticism simply led to another demerit in your dossier.

As it was implemented, the regulation became a total ban on any and all speakers deemed by officialdom to be "controversial." Meanwhile, the *Clarion-Ledger* and other keepers of the status quo kept pumping out their propaganda, so only one side could be heard.

At the outset of the 1966–67 school year, we submitted our list of proposed speakers to Dr. William Giles, our new university president (after Dr. Colvard left for North Carolina). Some proposed speakers were approved. Of those, the most outspoken was the homegrown white editor of the *Delta Democrat-Times*, Hodding Carter III (who later served as the Assistant Secretary of State for Public Affairs in the Jimmy Carter administration). His speech in November 1966 drew a near-capacity crowd in the YMCA auditorium, where he stated, "There must be something that Mississippi is doing wrong." He said the recent state elections (held earlier that month) were a "disgrace to the state, to the people, and to their needs," meaning that the real needs of Mississippians went unaddressed in campaigns that exclusively focused on segregationist politics, or, as it was commonly said, "Which candidate could 'out-nigger' the other."

Five of our proposed speakers were banned outright. We proposed Senator Ted Kennedy and, for balance, Governor George Wallace—both rejected as "too controversial." We also proposed to invite Bishop James Pike of Grace Cathedral in San Francisco—also rejected. He had often used his pulpit to attack organized religion for its racial and political views, and he allegedly had been accused of being "heretical" by some unnamed bishop. Nor were we allowed to bring in a nationally known infant-care expert. We wanted to help teenage moms, some of whom were MSU students, many of whom were ill-prepared to care for an infant. Dr. Peter Bertocci had given a lecture on the proper care of infants earlier at MSU but a prude in attendance thought he had described too graphically the proper way to wash and clean the genitals of a male infant. The administration used this incident to deny him another visit.

Most controversial of all: Aaron Henry, destined to become our cause célèbre. A black pharmacist who lived and practiced in Clarksdale, the home-grown Mississippian couldn't be mistaken for an "outside agitator." As president of the Mississippi NAACP, Henry remained a peaceful but persistent advocate of equal rights for blacks. As a result, his home and store had been shot up and their windows smashed by bricks. In May 1963, his drugstore was bombed, ripping a hole in the roof, but local officials claimed it had been hit by a bolt of lightning. In 1964, he had co-led the Mississippi Freedom Democratic Party's delegation to the Democratic National Convention in Atlantic City to challenge the all-white Mississippi Democratic Party delegation. In 1965, while leading a protest march, he was jailed in Clarksdale for parading without a permit, then chained to a garbage truck and forced to collect trash. In 1966, Aaron Henry stood as "the most likely candidate in Mississippi for the next Medgar Evers treatment," according to Professor James Silver in *Mississippi: The Closed Society*.

No black had ever given a speech at MSU—or any other white college in Mississippi—and the state board seemed determined to keep it that way. Aaron Henry was not trying to force his way to the microphone at MSU. White students wanted to hand him a microphone and to listen to what he had to say. No matter, the state board opposed a Henry visit and any other free exchange of ideas, especially when those ideas came from the NAACP.

At the Y, we were upset that an idea in and of itself could be deemed too hot to handle and wondered how the university could claim to provide academic freedom while suppressing the free exchange of ideas. On October 26, 1966, we penned a unanimous protest to the president of the university. In part, we stated:

> We of the YMCA Cabinet submit this letter in vigorous protest of your recent decision refusing Aaron Henry, Peter Bertocci, James Pike, Edward Kennedy and George Wallace the privilege of speaking on this campus. While we feel the gravity of this decision compels a formal reply, this letter is intended as an expression of concern from the Cabinet and does not question your convictions, integrity, or position.
>
> The YMCA Cabinet founds its protest in the truths that it is the function of a university to endorse a free society and not to oppose it, that an educated community can and should be free to exercise individual

judgment upon ideals, and that only through an exchange of ideas can men better understand each other.

To oppose a free academic society questions seriously our honor as a university. To deny the exchange of ideas is to deny the value of understanding our fellow men.

We believe that the political forces in this State which have turned citizen against citizen are the same forces which would exclude the rights of free men to enlarge their perspectives so as to mend these understandings. We further submit that ours is the time and the place which calls most urgently for genuine exchange of ideas for, if this generation of students is to overcome what others have perpetuated, then we must further the task of living with and not against our fellow citizens.

Everyone joined in the wordsmithing to ensure that we spoke with a unanimous voice. We seemed to be in constant session in our corner board room. I signed the protest as president and endorsed thereon the names of all cabinet members: Walter Dowdle, Debbie Davis, Garland Robertson, Judi Allen, Sam Love, Christine Thomas, Peggy Powell, Gil Brand, Tommy Tate, Frank Whittington, Faye Reeves, and Scott Wendelsdorf. Every one of these young men and women stood to be counted. At our meetings, we went over every sentence and heard out every motion to improve or soften any phrase. We weren't firebrands, just thirteen responsible students of all political stripes. There was no march or rally, simply a carefully composed letter, delivered to the university president, then published in the school newspaper.

In those days, elders in Mississippi were respected. To criticize them was "way out of line." Going on record as protestors, we ran the risk of being branded as troublemakers and could, at a minimum, prejudice later job opportunities. Despite this risk, we explained ourselves plainly, willing to go on record, viewing our protest as part of the deliberative process of academic freedom.

Our faculty board of advisors sent a parallel protest, but it was not unanimous. The faculty board protested the administration's "refusal to grant permission to the YMCA to invite to our campus Messrs. Henry,

Wallace, Pike, Bertocci and Kennedy." The board called it "a crippling blow to the promulgation on this campus of stimulating ideas and to that healthy exercise of open discussion which is the heart of a liberal education." Further, the board said, "We believe freedom is not served, but damaged, by the exclusion of decent men because of the possibility of strong protest by those whom they might offend. We believe with Jefferson that error cannot prevail if truth is free to combat it. And, the freedom of truth presupposes the freedom of error. We believe that the 'academic interest' can only suffer by any program of speakers selection which excludes men because of unpopularity, or of minority belief, or of fear of 'agitation.' Agitation is, in fact, essential to progress, as inertia is inimical to it."

The faculty protest was written by Dr. Robert Holland of the English department, who had served the YMCA and MSU for many years in his graceful and gentle way (as had his wife Pepper). A few faculty champions like Dr. Holland and Dr. Dick Haas, the folk-singing professor in the speech department, stood willing to put their name to a protest. So did Professor Sam Dudley, chairman of the speech department, and Professor John Davis, who wrote an op-ed piece in the school newspaper entitled "Speaker Ban at MSU." In challenging the ban, he wrote, "The only possible environment in which men and women may be trained for a free society is one in which all the rights of the men may be exercised." Professor Flavous Hutchinson stood up for the First Amendment, too.

In this moment of campus crisis, Cermette was called away for military service in Vietnam, so the support of these faculty members became all the more important to us.

Four members of our faculty advisory board voted against the protest. Across the campus at large, faculty members kept quiet out of fear of losing their jobs. Still lingering in the air was the wholesale purge of college professors by demagogue Governor Theodore Bilbo a few decades earlier. In fact, tenured liberal professors at Ole Miss law school who had spoken out against Governor Barnett's "interposition" rationale in the Meredith case had recently been forced out of the school. Rumors abounded—driven by the *Clarion-Ledger,* where columnist Tom Ethridge again attacked the MSU YMCA as being part of "the Revolution"—that state investigators would be sent in to root out the supposed communists who had infiltrated our campus. So, it wasn't surprising that almost half of our Y faculty board felt compelled to vote against our protest of the speaker ban. Nevertheless, Professor J. K. Bettersworth eventually wrote in *People's University*, "It was the campus YMCA that was destined to be the 'speakers' bad boy."

He should have included the campus Young Democrats as well.

In the darkness of Room 210 before we dozed off at night, Danny and I wondered what we could do? This question consumed us. It was so galling. While the YMCA cabinet and its faculty advisers composed inky thunderbolts and drew flak from the *Clarion-Ledger*, Danny, president of the MSU Young Democrats, came up with a more direct and dramatic idea—a challenge to the speaker ban in federal court.

Although the YMCA wished to present Aaron Henry, the YMCA itself would never have gone to court over it. We were too beholden to the university, and litigation would have appalled all of our faculty advisors, even the ones who had spoken out in favor of our protest. The Young Democrats, however, had no such constraints. The MSU chapter had also sought to sponsor Aaron Henry as a speaker. Unsurprisingly, the administration had also denied that request.

On Friday, October 7, Danny composed a memo and circulated it to the other MSU Young Democrats executive members (Turnage, Frank, and me). The memo proposed a lawsuit to challenge the state board's refusal to allow Aaron Henry to speak and called for a breakfast meeting on Thursday, October 11 at 7 a.m. in the cafeteria to reach a decision.

In that huge cathedral hall, mostly unattended at that early hour, the four of us sat at a square formica table in the middle of the north wing of the cafeteria. We, of course, remained steamed over the suppression of free speech, but what could really be done about it—or should be done about it—beyond our written protest? None of us had ever been in a courtroom, so the idea of actually going to court scared us. Suing under any circumstance was a huge step—with risks—but suing Mississippi and its officialdom would be even more perilous. We had less than a year left of our college careers. What if the state board, in reprisal, nitpicked our records to find ways to deny us diplomas? Maybe they would sabotage our applications to

*Aaron Henry speaking at the 1964 Democratic National Convention
(Courtesy of the Library of Congress)*

grad schools? Maybe they would put in a word at our draft boards? Would
we be forever branded as troublemakers and lose out on job opportunities?
Would reprisals be taken against the YMCA? Would threats rain down on
our faculty advisor, Flavous Hutchinson (as they eventually did)? Would
thugs attack us or our speaker as they had beaten our liberal guest a few
months earlier right in front of the Y?

As importantly, would suing place our families in jeopardy? Frank's dad,
in fact, soon refused to let him participate in any such lawsuit because it
would have jeopardized his business in Jackson. For his part, Danny's own
dad worked in a blue-collar job for the *Clarion-Ledger*, and one of its owners was on the very state board that had imposed the speaker ban. Bravely,
he told Danny "to do what was right and not to worry about him" and his
job. My own mother's job was safe, and she simply said, as she had with
the Earl Warren billboard, "You'd better be careful, son." (Willanna and her
husband, Ben, had moved out of state by then and were out of harm's way.)

If my dad had been alive, he would have said, "Son, you are there to
get an education. Don't jeopardize it by getting involved in politics. Your
teachers and officials have a school to run. They can't please everyone. You

should accept their decisions and move on. You are about to graduate. Stay focused on getting the best education you can. You have the rest of your life to get involved in politics. Straighten up and fly right." If he had been there and said that, it is likely that I would've acquiesced. But he was not, so I found my own way.

We had to make a difficult judgment call. Finally, after much worry, my own hesitation gave way to friendship and loyalty. Danny and I were close pals. He wanted to do this. I wanted to stand by him. Anyway, someone needed to challenge a clear-cut wrong. Who, if not us? For me, this became a merging moment of the accumulated influences of Willanna and my best pals; the progressive guidance of the YMCA and Cermette Clardy; the moderating effect of exposure to the rest of America via debating, and most of all, the moral force of the civil rights movement. Danny and I decided to go forward with litigation, meaning we would become named plaintiffs.

Danny had lined up a *pro bono* lawyer in Greenville through his contacts with the leadership of the Young Democrats. Even without legal training, we felt that it simply had to violate the First Amendment to bar Aaron Henry from appearing on a public campus to give a peaceful speech. In some way that I cannot now reconstruct, the American Civil Liberties Union gave us some advice, for I so stated in the letter quoted below (and Danny remembers it as well), but that ACLU advice, possibly given indirectly through an attorney, is now lost to history. To be clear, we were not trying to win monetary damages or profit personally—we just wanted to challenge the regulation used to suppress freedom of expression on campuses across the state. We wanted to stand up for everyone at MSU who wanted to hear someone like Aaron Henry speak.

Before suing, however, we decided to visit MSU President William Giles to explain ourselves, if for no other reason than to mitigate the ill will we anticipated from a lawsuit. A few days before our meeting, I wrote to President Giles. My letter, dated October 23, said, among other things:

> The American Civil Liberties Union has confirmed the Young
> Democrats' suspicion that the denial of these speakers is clearly a viola-
> tion of Constitutional principles. It seems only natural that an educated

community could sit in rational judgment of any view—no matter how radical. It is an insult to the University to deny it that honor. It hurts me, as I have said, to not be able to hear, for example, Aaron Henry explain the Negro vote. . . . It hurts me to know that there are those who restrict academic inquiry—into any aspect of man's life. Those who claim political speakers should be banned are the same who would have the citizenry uneducated on political issues.

As an officer of the Young Democrats Club, I have participated in the decision to seek a remedy to this situation regarding the recent refusal by your office of Mr. Aaron Henry, the man whom the Governor of this State termed the most responsible Negro in Mississippi. As a last resort of direct action, I am afraid that this will mean federal court action.

One reason for my letter was to make clear that in joining the proposed lawsuit over the speaker ban, I was doing so as an officer of the Young Democrats, not as president of the student YMCA. I wanted to reduce the risk of retribution against the YMCA. I had been wearing two hats, one for the YMCA and its letter of protest, and one as an officer of the Young Democrats, threatening formal action in federal court. The letter to Dr. Giles tried to make clear the distinction, for whatever good it might do, which turned out to be not much. Another reason for my letter was the slim hope that the administration might relent and allow Aaron Henry to speak after all, a hope that had more purchase than I had anticipated.

At our meeting with Dr. Giles in his Lee Hall office, it was just the three of us—Danny, Dr. Giles, and me. We remained calm and respectful, although it felt to Danny and me like a scene from *High Noon*. Ever gracious, Dr. Giles began with his compliments on our debating achievements for MSU, thus making us feel like ingrates for causing him trouble. After thanking him for hearing us, we said that the rejection of Aaron Henry violated academic freedom. Surprisingly, President Giles agreed. He said if it were up to him, Aaron Henry would be welcomed, but his hands remained tied by the state board of trustees, who had ordered him to reject the Henry application. We broached the potential lawsuit in the most polite way we could. We said that we felt strongly about the right of students to hear Aaron Henry and that we felt the issue should be decided by a federal judge rather than the state board of trustees. Furthermore, we said that we had a *pro bono* lawyer lined up, ready to go, and that we wished to tell President Giles in advance, as a personal courtesy to him, that we would seek a federal ruling. He thanked us politely, noting that everyone had to follow his own conscience. The meeting lasted about twenty minutes.

At least some of us in the Young Democrats felt determined to file a lawsuit, but before we had begun to prepare it, word came from President Giles. He said he had passed on our intentions to the board of trustees and, on his advice and in light of our threatened lawsuit, the board had reversed itself. Now Aaron Henry could give his speech on campus. Astounding! We had won, without having to go to court. Almost all of us felt proud of Dr. Giles and his courage to push back against the establishment. We did not yet know of the retribution to come.

The reversal launched a storm of vitriol in the Jackson press. In a *Clarion-Ledger* column entitled "Controversy Over Speakers at MSU," Tom Ethridge wrote:

> The YMCA at Mississippi State University has made itself controversial by inviting five guest speakers to appear before groups at different times—against the wishes of MSU President W. L. Giles.
>
> He has backed down and withdrawn his ban against their visits, under threat of a lawsuit by campus "Young Democrats" who insist that their fellow Democrat, State NAACP President Aaron Henry, be allowed to speak, as scheduled.
>
> IT BOILS DOWN to a small group using threats to overrule MSU authority and nullify official policy of our State Board of Trustees.

With the headlines that Aaron Henry would be coming after all, considerable anticipation mounted. It would be the first speech ever given by a black at a traditionally white state college or university in Mississippi. Everyone knew history was unfolding before our eyes.

33

The First Black Speaker on a White Campus in Mississippi

O n the evening of Tuesday, January 10, 1967, we could feel the change in the air. Thanks to all the publicity and controversy, the YMCA auditorium jammed to overflowing well before the speech was to begin. To our surprise, more than seven hundred attendees clamored to cram into a hall that would hold four hundred. As the massive overflow became clear, the university did a good deed and let us move the event to Lee Hall, the largest auditorium on campus. George Verrall, our YMCA dorm daddy and elder statesman, helped make this happen at the last minute. One of us took to the microphone to direct everyone across the street. As Danny and I walked alongside Aaron Henry in a sea of whites migrating in the early evening darkness, it occurred to us that we had naively taken no security precautions to protect our guest from an assault. He was vulnerable at that moment, just as Mr. Kelley had been a few months earlier when two thugs beat him unconscious in front of the Y. We passed by the site of the earlier attack. Thankfully, no incident occurred. Everyone got across safely to Lee Hall.

When the buzz died down, Danny, as president of the MSU Young Democrats, and Joe, as vice president, sat on the stage with Henry. I sat in the audience about ten rows back on the left side of the auditorium. Danny came forward to welcome everyone and to introduce Henry, who took the lectern to polite applause. That polite welcome came as a relief, for we had worried over possible hecklers. In a speech entitled "Negro Voting in Mississippi," Henry spoke on the Voting Rights Act of 1965, then still fresh. He began by expressing appreciation for an opportunity to "make his witness in the cause of freedom." He explained the bloody history of denials of voting rights in Mississippi and the need for federal protection. He explained the likely impact of the Voting Rights Act on future elections in Mississippi. He said that he felt "a new wind blowing—a wind that will sound frightening to some because it will blow away their evil system." (The Voting Rights Act, indeed, proved to have a tremendous impact on elections in Mississippi.) He added, "If we work together and die together on foreign soil for the cause of democracy, then why can't we here? If we join hands then, we can go forward." He argued that people had to be taught to hate and that the hate in our state would stop when the teaching of hate stopped.

Henry invited questions. Someone in the audience asked whether all of this would lead to interracial marriage, whereupon Aaron Henry said he would like to put that one "to bed right away," which drew a large laugh from the audience. He said blacks wanted to come to the best schools in the state to get the best education, not just to get a date. When asked how he felt about being the first Negro to speak at MSU (indeed, at any "white" college in Mississippi), he commented, "I have been on quite a few campuses all over the country and this is one of the warmest receptions I have ever gotten." He was an accomplished speaker and looked at home on the stage, projecting poise, sincerity, and resolve.

At the end, a tiny group of faculty led by speech department chair Sam Dudley, all sitting front row center, rose to invite a standing ovation. Professor Dudley was a stalwart of the faculty willing to be counted. Then, slowly, most everyone else in the hall stood and joined in the ovation, a sustained one. It was most respectful, a happy ending to a historic moment on the MSU campus. (There were no boos.) The entire event, start to finish, remained peaceful and a model of civil dialogue in an era of tumult.

Two days later, on January 12, Tom Ethridge's column criticized the Aaron Henry event as well as the Young Democrats and the YMCA:

> The LEADER of the state's NAACP organization, Aaron Henry of Clarksdale, became the first Negro to speak at Mississippi State University when he addressed a student group Tuesday night, sponsored by an integrationist splinter outfit calling itself the Young Mississippi Democrats.

Jan 13, 1967 ~~~~~ - AARON HENRY SPEAKS -
SC, Miss.   Two nights ago, Aaron Henry, president
7 the NAACP, was the first Negro speaker to
speak to the student body. There was so
large a turn-out that the program
had to be moved to Lee Hall (from
the YMCA) in order to seat them. His
address was on "Negro Voting in Mississippi,"
and contained a very thought-provoking
section of content which said, "You got to
be taught to hate...." This is true at

The beginning of my journal entry on Aaron Henry's speech

It reportedly has been financed by Bobby Kennedy and other New
Frontier radicals.

A noteworthy angle is that Aaron Henry's visit was first arranged by
the campus YMCA which invited other controversial speakers unwanted
as guests by the MSU president.

IT'S BEING ASKED why the YMCA has become a party to honoring
Henry and embarrassing MSU's administration by helping force a change
in policy on speakers.

State leaders and boosters of the YMCA should look into this, some
suggest, because the Aaron Henry episode at MSU is not exactly a boost
for YMCA prestige. The agency exists by public contributions on the as-
sumption it is non-controversial.

Sensitive Mississippians may not be able to do anything about the civil
rights angle, but they can do something about the YMCA—if it becomes
identified as an instrument of the "Revolution."

One anonymous letter to the editor of our student newspaper blasted
Aaron Henry as an undesirable, but two letters to the editor were favorable
and signed. One was Danny's:

Tuesday night in Lee Hall, a Negro Civil Rights leader spoke to the

Student Body of a Mississippi University for the first time in history. The ideas he advocated were not new, but the fact that they were presented is significant.

The Student Body of MSU responded not only in large number, but in mature consideration for his position. Probably very few agreed in whole to what Aaron Henry said, but they listened. The questions that followed, for the most part, were sensible and reasonable.

It is education in its finest form when students respond above and beyond that which is required of them in classrooms and to hear and question ideas and philosophies that may be totally alien to them. Those who did hear Aaron Henry should be congratulated for their willingness to do what so many don't—and that is to listen to the other side.

The other letter was mine. In the *Clarion-Ledger*, as quoted above, Tom Ethridge had criticized the whole episode and suggested that the campus YMCA was becoming part of "the Revolution." In response, I replied with a letter to the editor of our campus newspaper:

> As president of the MSU-YMCA, I cannot let the caustic words of Mr. Tom Ethridge's recent *Clarion-Ledger* column condemning our organization go unchallenged. The purpose of this statement is to challenge the highly negative philosophy underwritten by Mr. Ethridge.
>
> The philosophy of this editor is as he stated—that the YMCA should not be controversial. This we of the YMCA Cabinet cannot accept in the environment in which we find ourselves, for there are very extreme conditions of which we are very aware which cannot be squarely met in a framework of non-controversy.
>
> Aaron Henry said last Tuesday that "you've got to be taught to hate." Tom Ethridge and his newspaper have taught hate for more years than most people have lived. Because of the leadership his colleagues and political friends have given Mississippi, our citizenry has been divided, we have fought against each other and in this confusion and hate we have managed rather well to remain at the bottom of every significant indicator in America.

Controversy is not the issue. The issue is: "What are we doing to make a better society?" We of the Cabinet pledge that as long as Mr. Ethridge or his likes continue to divide our people, we as Christians at Mississippi State will be no less controversial in changing our neighbors as was Christ in changing the World.

No one ever physically threatened me or Danny or anyone else on campus over the Aaron Henry affair. The students and faculty treated it as a historic occasion or at least took it in stride. The administration kept quiet at first. While the *Clarion-Ledger* continued a stream of criticisms, no violence ever came of it.

Danny should receive full credit for his driving role at the helm of the MSU Young Democrats. Had it not been for his leadership, stubbornness, and courage, we would have graduated still waiting for the first speech by an African American on a white campus in Mississippi.*

ALTHOUGH THE HENRY SPEECH wound up being a Young Democrat event, the YMCA gave full support. We were pleased with the historic outcome and how it fit in with our other Y programs. We had a tutoring program, a free university course called "Poverty in Mississippi" (our local version of the "plunge" in Chicago), a radio program on whether China should be admitted to the United Nations, and a "coffee house" in Starkville that was, as was true for hip coffee houses of the era, a nighttime music club and hangout. Our speaker's program continued with other guests, such as Frederic Holt, who had served in our embassy in Saigon and who spoke on the Vietnam war, a talk we arranged to have broadcast live on WSSO, our local radio station.

A glow surrounded the YMCA. The heavens seemed in harmony. It was most satisfying to relax with friends on that massive porch overlooking the main street through campus or to gather for the evening news in the lobby

---

* One account has given me a larger role in this story than I deserve. An academic article devoted to the history of the speaker ban at MSU focused too much on the letter I wrote. Gregory J. Griffin, "Speakers' Rights, Censorship, and the Death of God: The Struggle for Free Speech at Mississippi State University," *Journal of Mississippi History* LXVII (Winter 2005).

with the realization that we had taken a small step forward for our state. We were doing good. The student body and faculty largely appreciated us. John D. Rockefeller would have thought his money had been well spent.

On the large porch of the Y, Camilla and I propped our feet up on a sunny afternoon in early spring. Just in front of us, a loud car raced by on University Drive going way too fast. "Keep on a'going, Brother; Hell's a'open all night," Camilla said in her lilting voice verging always on laughter, pretending to be her grandmother uttering a vintage Mississippi line. Our smiles that afternoon reflected our positive and satisfying spirit. We kidded each other about our foibles. She was saying her farewells, for she had decided that Vietnam called her. She had graduated early and had enlisted in the American Red Cross as a freelance journalist, and by the end of March she would be immersed in her next challenge, half a world away.

34

Reprisals

Those *Clarion-Ledger* attacks on the YMCA grew legs, and the pressure was on to clean out the hotbed of troublemakers in the YMCA dorm. On March 2 Ethridge's column, referring to Aaron Henry, stated:

> SOME FEEL that the question of propriety is especially valid when a speaker generally considered as an agitator—and who has been convicted in a state court on a morals charge—is invited to be a guest of honor at YMCA-sponsored meeting at a tax-supported school.

The crackdown came. Nothing could be done to the MSU Young Democrats. The group had no assets, no financing, and only a few members. But the YMCA had plenty to lose. And the long-entrenched, conservative dean of students set about to make sure we lost it all.

The dean told the student Y cabinet that (1) the YMCA dorm residents would all have to move out at the end of the semester and a new philosophy and religion department would then use our vacated rooms for office space, (2) a new YMCA head (to replace Cermette and not yet found) would be subservient to the new philosophy and religion department, (3) there would be no faculty advisory board any longer, and (4) YMCA financing from the university via student fees would stop. The administration further decided to strip the YMCA of its right to invite speakers on campus and to consolidate "the speaker program" in the hands of the student union and a faculty-student committee, according to Professor Bettersworth in *People's University*.

We were thunderstruck.

For whatever good it did, our student cabinet voted eleven to nothing to reject the proposal. We revised and strengthened our mission statement—drafted carefully by Walter Dowdle, our vice president—to clearly articulate the Christian purpose behind our program. The school newspaper ran stories on the crackdown. Editorials came out in support of the Y and its mission. Student letters protested the action by the administration. A student survey found that, by a ratio of 60 to 5, students thought the YMCA served a Christian purpose (with 35 percent undecided) and by a ratio of 56 to 11 they thought the YMCA served a "real need on campus" (with 33 percent undecided). A spontaneous student meeting was held to "save the YMCA." On March 13, the Y cabinet met with President Giles to seek his help, but no agreement was reached. Cermette remained in Vietnam—in no position to help us.

The reprisals violated the Rockefeller stipulation for the construction of the YMCA building in 1914 that the building would be "forever devoted to the social and religious uses of the students" and that "the conduct of the work in said building, subject to the discipline of the College, shall be under the direction of the Young Men's Christian Association." Such legal details seemed of little concern to the administration.

What was really going on was a plan to drive a stake through the heart of the progressive student YMCA administration. Although retaliation against the YMCA had been an ever-present risk during the battle against the speaker ban, I had not appreciated the full scope of retribution we might face. One of the reasons I wrote the October letter to Dr. Giles was to make clear that my participation in the lawsuit would be solely in my capacity as an officer of the Young Democrats. Had I known what was in store for the Y, it would have given me even more pause; certainly I would have had more discussions within the YMCA leadership. But in the actual event, not a single YMCA member criticized our course—and most applauded it. The YMCA had stood up and publicly protested an evil system. Now, the evil system had struck back.

In May 1967, Danny and I finished our college graduation requirements and closed the door to Room 210 one last time. With it closed a proud chapter in MSU history. The dorm was cleaned out, never again to be used for student purposes. Even today, the underused building persists as a requiem for a vibrant era at the university, one cut short by official retribution.

ANOTHER REPRISAL CAME. PROFESSOR Hutchinson had warned Danny and me that Tom Ethridge was going to run a series of columns in the Mississippi paper on "communists on campus," all to be used in the gubernatorial race that summer. An Ethridge column in the *Clarion-Ledger* on February 22, 1967, called for an "official inquiry" into academic freedom and the Young Democrats:

> BEFORE IT'S OVER, the 1967 gubernatorial race may find "academic freedom" becoming a hot issue. Some observers feel it has been grossly abused.
>
> Some are in favor of an official inquiry into the so-called "Young Democrats of Mississippi" organization—a phone-booth size splinter group reportedly financed in part by left-wing elements of the Great Society.

He went on to blast the Young Democrats and the concept of academic freedom:

> CRITICISM OF lax administrative discipline has been manifested in various quarters, especially with regard to so-called "Young Democrat" clubs on tax-supported campuses apparently trying to control administrative policy in some phases.
>
> YDC threats to sue MSU's president for violating their "civil rights" have been resented by many taxpayers and school patrons.
>
> WITH DUE RESPECT for zeal and "academic freedom," it would seem that students automatically agree and accept the authority of a college administration when they enroll. If and as that authority becomes unacceptable, students should leave—and good riddance.
>
> The idea of youngsters taking a college president into court for exercising his authority strikes us as ridiculously far-fetched arrogance.

What about that "official inquiry" Ethridge referenced? In my last semester at MSU, soon after Ethridge's column was printed, our first and longtime neighbor on Terry Road, Mrs. Edna Brown, told my mother that two investigators from the State Sovereignty Commission had recently visited her one day and asked questions about me, my activities, and my plans after graduation. She told them that the subject of their investigation lived right next door and they ought to go down and ask him directly if they really wanted to know. Mrs. Brown was a conservative, but she hung tough, loved our family, and wanted no part of any scare tactics. So, she let Mother know. I talked to Mrs. Brown, and she told me the whole story. Thanking her, I then visited Junior's mom (our only other close neighbor), and she anxiously told me that she, too, had been visited by Commission investigators. Mrs. Feild then began to sob, too terrified to tell me how the conversation had gone. The investigators, of course, did not drop by and ask any questions at our home. They wanted simply to intimidate our family by upsetting our neighbors.*

---

* In 2012, I reviewed the files of the Commission posted online (pursuant to a federal court decree) and was unable to find any file or reference to my name. The archivist, however, told me that the online files remained incomplete. (I did see, however, a reference to an investigative file on Danny from 1974, dwelling on his membership in the ACLU.)

35

Riding the Wind

College was over. Not only had we received an education, as our parents had wanted, but a good one, thanks to underpaid professors and mentors like Wayne Gaddis, Brad Bishop, and Cermette Clardy. The rigors of engineering and math were destined to add discipline to my analysis in law school. Debating had given me the ability to stand on my feet to present a case. Most of all, MSU had become a defining moment for me. In retrospect, I wouldn't trade those four years for anything. But back then, when graduation rolled around I remained bitter about the reprisals for our fight against the speaker ban, so I skipped the diploma ceremony.

That summer, at the annual convention of the National Council of Student YMCAs in Cleveland, I attended as a national vice president (having been elected in Chicago the previous year) and was elevated to national president for the next year. Suzan Caldwell, a pretty blonde from California, came from UCLA as a representative of the Pacific Southwest Region. She was elected as national vice president. It was love at first sight. She proved perfect for me. That led to a courtship at the expense of the national YMCA; we saw each other almost monthly at our national officer meetings. After a summer job for me with a solo law practitioner in Beverly Hills (which Suzan helped arrange), we married at summer's end. We have been very happily married since—fifty years in 2018—with two wonderful children, Allison and John. That's how I hit a home run—a walk-off.

36

A Tank Commander

I'm meeting with Dixon Pyles in Jackson. It's the summer of 1970. Pyles and his partner, Betty Tucker, are among the very few homegrown white lawyers in Mississippi who will represent labor unions and blacks. For that, you had to be tough. During World War Two, Dixon commanded a tank in Europe, on Utah Beach, at Bastogne, and in between. He's definitely tough. He's also short, bald, and garrulous, with black horn-rimmed glasses. He's well-liked by the local conservative bar despite his liberal views. I'm seeking advice on how a young law student like me could hope to eventually break into the Jackson market.

"I keep them in business—that's why they like me," he holds forth. "But it wasn't always like that, let me tell you. No, sir. When I went to Crystal Springs to help organize a plant—that was in 1950—the chamber of commerce met me like a lynch mob at the train station and said, 'Mr. Pyles, you're not welcome here. You better just get on over to that other platform and take the train back to Jackson.' I told them, 'Thank you, I will do just that.' So, I got on the train back to Jackson, went straight to the federal court, got a restraining order under the National Labor Relations Act, went right back to Crystal Springs that afternoon, and served the order on those bastards as I got off the train."

His eyes sparkle and his face beams. I smile wide. It's a good story. Dixon's full of them, most of them about the "economic royalists," as he calls them, and how he's taken them on.

Next, he tells me about his civil rights class action. He is suing the City of Jackson on behalf of all the black sanitation workers, hundreds of them, none of whom has ever gotten promoted to a supervisor or driver; all of those positions remain in white hands. Would I help him long distance, he asks, with some legal research after I return to law school in the fall?

"Sure," I say, not knowing if he means *pro bono* or money *bono*. Either way, it sounds important. (Eventually, he will generously pay me more than my work is worth.)

"I just took the deposition," he continues, "of one of the leading lights over there at City Hall and asked him, 'Sir, isn't it a fact that the City of Jackson has practiced race discrimination against Negroes in employment all the way back to the Civil War?' And you know what he said? 'Yes, sir, Mr. Pyles, that's true.' He was proud of it. Young man, with evidence like that, we can't lose this case in a federal court, even in Mississippi."

37

More Assassinations

During my first year in law school, Dr. King died by gunfire in Memphis on April 4, 1968. The world had known that his life remained in constant danger, but still we were stunned—an incomparable leader, our nation's conscience—cruelly cut down. A spontaneous candlelight march through Harvard Square followed that night. Suzan happened to be visiting me at law school, and we carried candles in the march along Massachusetts Avenue.

Back at MSU, Frank Whittington and the remnants of the Y program wore black armbands and stood at the statue of Stephen D. Lee in the center of campus, handing out a written call for the campus to gather at the chapel that evening to pause and reflect on the violence of the era and the loss of Dr. King. Some students wadded up the notices and tossed them in the trash. The observance went forward only to have a rock thrown through the chapel window and an intruder sing "Dixie."

For our HH newsletter, on April 12, 1968, Danny wrote these words in memory of Dr. King:

> As it did nationwide, the brutal death of Martin Luther King, Jr., brought to focus in the South once again the naked fact that man today in this nation still tries to resolve problems, events, or ill-feelings with violence. The problem is age-old and basic, and the public sounded outrage of such events as in Memphis or Dallas seem to disappear after a few months. The progressive south was shocked; the repressive south was self-righteously saying "he brought it on himself." The rationalization was

183

made that it was only one man who committed the act, but the attitudes were prevalent.

The death will give momentum to the civil rights struggle for decent housing, jobs, and equal opportunity, just as President Kennedy's death helped in the passage of his programs in the Congress. Streets will be named after Dr. King, monuments will rise in his honor, and guilt-ridden city administrators will look again at the plight of the Negro and take steps again to give him hope, but the basic attitude will remain. Months later or years later, a man espousing controversial causes will die by hidden men who have been encouraged even so slightly by us when we fail to object to injustice, bigotry, and hate, that is in existence in this most civilized society.

A few weeks later, Robert Kennedy was gunned down in Los Angeles. With the same eloquence, Danny wrote for our newsletter. His concluding paragraph is still painful to read forty years later:

> Robert Kennedy is dead. He died seeking the highest office in America. It was Robert Kennedy whom I had grown to respect and admire more than any other man. As a father, as a government leader, as a master politician, even as a Christian, Robert Kennedy lived his life to the fullest. Perhaps only posterity will recognize his complete significance. In my mind there was no doubt that his full potential had not been reached.
>
> Perhaps a new vigor may be brought to America, but I can't see it. A new leader may speak to America, but I can't hear him. A new direction may come to politics, but I can't feel it. Indeed, a new chance may come to America, but I wonder if we deserve it.

All of us who had placed our faith in King and the Kennedys felt immense pain and disillusionment. Yet we were young, and even in a few short years, we had already seen progress. Wouldn't more progress come if we'd follow their examples? That became our solace.

38

Danny Brings the First Amendment to Mississippi

In 1968, while a law student at Ole Miss, Danny went on to directly challenge the speaker regulation by the board of trustees. The Young Democrats again wished to invite a black speaker to campus, and the board of trustees again said no. Danny enlisted a young Harvard Law grad, Jimmy Robertson of Greenville, to represent him. (Robertson was destined for later service on the Mississippi Supreme Court.) This time, Danny went to court, and a three-judge panel—including Judge William Keady—invalidated the speaker regulations for all colleges and universities throughout the state. Years later, Danny was introduced to Judge Keady at a luncheon, and Keady said, "Yes, I remember Danny. He and I brought the First Amendment to Mississippi."

While that lawsuit remained underway, the speaker ban persisted at MSU. There, the YMCA and the Young Democrats were denied permission to invite Charles Evers to speak at MSU. Debbie Davis, by then the first woman president of the YMCA, and others drove to Greenville to participate in Danny's lawsuit. Charles Evers finally came to MSU and spoke to a packed house at Dorman Hall in March of 1970.

One villain of the speaker-ban saga was the Board of Trustees of the Mississippi State Institutions of Higher Learning. This fact is illustrated by a letter penned by its chairman at the time. M. M. Roberts was an attorney, the entrenched board of trustees chairman, and an unrepentant racist. In 1970, just after Evers spoke at MSU, Roberts wrote a letter to other members of the board concerning a federal court hearing over whether black speakers would be allowed at the University of Mississippi and at MSU. Roberts's letter speaks volumes about what Mississippi was like in those times:

> The judge ordered the appearance of this Negro to speak. One of the interesting things was that this President of the Young Democrats testified that they were going to have an unusual luncheon for Charles Evers before he spoke at 7:30 last night. I know they enjoyed it. I hope he smelled like Negroes usually do.
>
> Somehow, I wish it were so that we could clean house for those who do not understand Mississippi and its ways of life, but I guess this is expecting too much of our Board. If I had my way, we would have one rule about speakers and that is that no one would be permitted on any campus of any school in this State except those who appear for classroom teaching. If I had my way, we would stop using funds collected from students for the operation of student newspapers. My information is that a sophomore Negro has a prominent place on the student newspaper staff, at Mississippi State. Somehow, I cannot believe that Mississippi State is no longer a cow college. It is controlled by the influx of foreign ideologies, maybe city slickers.

These hateful words, written by a state official, epitomize a prevailing attitude in Mississippi—a most hostile attitude toward blacks as well as toward free speech.

But Charles Evers finally was heard at MSU, more than five years after Danny and I made that heartfelt visit in December 1964, sat in what had been Medgar's office, extended our condolences, and asked him if he would come and speak at MSU.

39

Back Home in Mississippi

During law school, Suzan and I made a decision to return to Mississippi after graduation. To that end, in the summer of 1970, I worked for the Mississippi Research and Development Center in Jackson. That August, Allison was born in St. Dominic's Hospital, where Mother served as the head obstetrics nurse. Jack and Ron visited the proud parents at the hospital, but no one was prouder than Mother. She was a grandmother (yet again)—better still, her own ward had brought Allison into the world. Mother had sold 2325 Terry Road while I was in law school. She now lived in a modern home on the upscale side of town, closer to the hospital. At the end of the summer, our young family returned to Cambridge.

In my last year at Harvard, Justice William O. Douglas selected me as one of his three law clerks for the 1971–72 Supreme Court term, an unexpected opportunity that arose after the justice decided to take on a graduate of Harvard's joint law-public policy program as a law clerk. The joint program, which issues degrees from Harvard Law School as well as the Kennedy School of Government, was established while I was at Harvard, and I was a member of its first class. Completing the joint degree meant spending an extra year in Cambridge. There were only three of us in that first class of the joint program, so only three of us were eligible for the clerkship opportunity. Judge Charles Clark of the United States Court of Appeals, sitting in Jackson, had just selected me for an upcoming clerkship, but when he heard about the Douglas opportunity, he immediately, firmly, even cheerfully, insisted that I try for it. All three members of that first joint program graduating class interviewed for the clerkship. I got the job! Thanks to Judge Clark's graciousness, I became privileged to assist Justice Douglas in the Abortion Cases and the so-called "Trees Have Standing" case, among others.

Justice Douglas was particularly generous in giving a white kid from Mississippi the benefit of the doubt and refusing to stereotype. At Harvard, by contrast, I had sensed reservation from my classmates (but not the faculty) upon learning of my roots. Students were cautious, wanting to avoid associating with someone who might turn out to be a closet racist. In time, I made close friends at Harvard, despite the fact that in those days many Northerners indulged that presumption. Justice Douglas and his wife, Cathy, however, gave me a fair chance.

After the clerkship, our little family moved to Jackson and bought a small house. By that point, Danny had married the ever-gracious Sharon Miller, a college teacher he had met while attending law school at Ole Miss, and the dream envisioned in Room 210 came true in July 1972, when Danny and I were admitted to practice and went in with Dixon Pyles and his partner, Betty Tucker, in Jackson.

We were practicing law! Together!

Right after the Second World War, Dixon had represented Willie McGee, a black man accused of raping a white woman in Laurel, Mississippi. The all-white jury deliberated for a matter of minutes before issuing their guilty verdict. Dixon won a reversal on appeal due to the exclusion of blacks from the jury. A civil rights group hired a new lawyer to represent McGee in the next trial, which led to a conviction and a death sentence. In 1951, McGee was executed in Mississippi's "traveling electric chair." The execution was broadcast live on the radio.

Betty ranked as one of the first woman attorneys in Mississippi. Her specialty was workers' compensation. She volunteered that her father had been a steamboat captain on the Mobile River. She remained ever devoted to Dixon. Her office walls were yellowed from her constant smoking. She later became one of Mississippi's first woman judges.

In my law school years, Dixon and Betty had hired me to work

I took this photo of Danny Cupit and Dixon Pyles digesting a case in 1972

long-distance on a civil rights case against the City of Jackson. It became a class action suit in federal court on behalf of all black sanitation workers seeking relief against race discrimination in promotions. Every driver remained white. No "can-handler" (they all were black) had ever been promoted to driver. It became, I believe, the first civil rights class action suit ever filed by homegrown white lawyers in Mississippi on behalf of African Americans. When we returned to Jackson, I continued on the same case, *Local 1888, AFSCME v. City of Jackson,* and I argued our major summary judgment motion before United States District Judge Dan Russell in Gulfport. Ours was a powerful motion, for the city officials had admitted—even proudly—in depositions that yes, indeed, they had practiced race discrimination in hiring and promotion dating all the way back to the Civil War.

Judge Russell never ruled on the motion. The record of discrimination was too strong for him to rule against us, so he just sat on it. Eventually, the United States Department of Justice intervened, which led to a class settlement (after I left) with a handsome cash award for each class member. In the same case, I also argued an appeal on an interlocutory issue before the United States Court of Appeals for the Fifth Circuit, an appeal the city won.

Suzan and I borrowed one thousand dollars a month to live on, a bank line of credit that Dixon had arranged for us; the firm was not turning a profit while I was there. Dixon told me to be patient, that eventually we would hit big on a case. But, in the meantime, Suzan and I had nothing to fall back on. I was the only breadwinner, but I wasn't winning any bread. We had house payments and our daughter to support. Federal judges in our district rarely granted much in attorney's fees in civil rights cases, even in the strongest of them. The financial stress became too much. I needed a paying job. I asked Suzan where she wanted to go. She instantly replied "California" (where her parents lived). That was December 1972, the hardest decision of my life—giving up on a dream and leaving Mississippi—for good.

Danny would have to become our Atticus Finch.

Suzan, Allison, John, and me at home with our dog, Sandy (2003)

40

Mississippi in the Sierra

It's August 2010. My Mississippi pals and I are taking in the twilight after a hard day of backpacking in the Sierra. Dinner is over and the cleanup done—time to relax and talk. Jack Purvis offers that our freeze-dried dinners compare favorably to Army MREs, a comment that leads him to reminisce about the routines of Army life.

"Jack, tell us what Vietnam was really like for you," Walter Dowdle asks, his gaze turning serious. This has been on all of our minds, including the mind of my son, John, now twenty-four.

Butts on the ground and jackets zipped in the cool of the evening, we settle back on glacier-smoothed boulders. Scotch is allowed but no campfire—we love the wilderness too much for that.

Matter of factly, Jack tells the whole experience chronologically, starting with his basic training, then officer training, then helicopter flight school. The narrative eventually leads to Vietnam and a forward operations base where he commanded a Huey. One day, word came that some American flyers went down in enemy territory. Jack got assigned to go in and rescue them. After a long flight, Jack located them, then hovered down through a hole in the jungle canopy just wide enough to clear the rotor. Staying only a few inches off the ground, Jack and his crew got the flyers aboard, then, with surgical precision, lifted skyward, taking enemy fire all the while. They got back, all safe.

It's hard to know what to say after a story like that.

"Did they," Kirk Shaw finally asks, "give you a medal for that?"

There's a long pause.

"The Bronze Star," Jack answers.

He could add, but doesn't, *for valor.*

Jack continues with another story, a choice between life and death. As part of a humanitarian mission, he and an enlisted man landed one morning outside a remote village to pick up a young boy with a cleft palate to transport him for repair surgery by Army doctors. They approached the village on foot via a narrow bridge. A quarter of the way across, they saw a lone teenager—probably from the village, dressed in black pajamas, the Viet Cong uniform, and carrying an AK-47—entering the bridge from the other side, coming their way. They were the only three on the bridge.

The enlisted man, carrying an Army-issue M-16, said, "Captain, what do you want me to do?"

As they closed in at a brisk pace, Jack—Captain Purvis—had only moments to decide. Nothing in the manual covered this.

In the safety of our Sierra camp, all of us ponder what in the hell we would have done on that bridge. Then Jack tells us the order he gave.

"Keep on walking, just as we are."

They passed the VC, all weapons held but unaimed. They looked over their shoulders to watch him continue on.

Another silence. In the wilderness, silence is pure.

"How'd you decide on that, Jack?" Sidney finally asks.

Jack whisks in the air through his teeth, his way of beginning a considered thought.

"The military," Jack answers, "is about missions. I figured all of us on that bridge that day were on mission, and no mission involved killing someone. That teenager's mission was to catch up with his unit. Our mission was humanitarian. The village elders had probably spread the word about our purpose. We stayed on mission, and he stayed on mission."

The young boy got his palate fixed, thanks to Captain Purvis and American military surgeons.

Decades later, stars shine over the Sierra. All of us are as proud as we can be of Captain Purvis.

41

Willanna

It's August 2013. We're on the Tioga Pass Road in the Yosemite backcountry heading for a trailhead hostel. We're about to begin the next of what have come to be known as the annual "Mississippi Trips," four- or five-day backpacking trips in the Sierra with my Mississippi pals, all of whom have gone on to contribute mightily to our country. The ascendant Rim Fire is exploding on our left, eight miles distant, soon to become the most destructive Sierra fire in history. We stop high at a lookout just shy of White Wolf to take in the sweep and breadth of the inferno—a panorama of gray, brown billows towering over thirty thousand feet.

My cell phone vibrates.

I can see it's Willanna's number, but the signal goes dead.

The news must be bad. Earlier, Suzan and I had gone to visit Willanna in North Carolina after the terrible news of her cancer. Afterward, we had talked by phone weekly.

Two hours later, at our trailhead hostel in Tuolumne Meadows, I try Ben, Willanna's husband.

"I can hear you, Ben, go ahead." It's a spotty connection.

"Willanna died this morning," Ben gets out. "She went peacefully. She's gone now. We want you to know."

This news had to come, but, still, I am thunderstruck.

He continues, "Leah and the boys are with me."

I ask about a memorial service. Willanna insisted, he says, that none be held (but we will hold one anyway in November). That night, at the trail-head hostel, Willanna appears in a vivid dream. Looking young and fit, in perfect health, she smiles. "I love you, Bill. It's better than you think. I am with Mom and Dad and Pop." I reply, "I love you, Willanna."

Our mother and father taught us decency and fairness. Willanna taught us to fight for what was right.

42

What Became of Us

After Suzan and I left Jackson, I found work at Morrison & Foerster in San Francisco, an excellent firm, and was fortunate to spend almost all of my career there as a trial lawyer (except for two years when Jimmy Carter was president to serve as an Assistant to the Solicitor General in Washington). Suzan eventually enjoyed a career teaching in the Oakland public schools and is now retired. She gets all the credit for our two accomplished and fun children, Allison and John, both now successful, for our lovely home and garden, and for just about everything else that makes a marriage work a long time.

After twenty-five years as a trial lawyer at Morrison & Foerster, I was appointed by President Bill Clinton to be a federal district judge in San Francisco, where I still serve. The seat I filled had been occupied by the Honorable Thelton Henderson. In 1963, he had been the first black attorney ever hired by the Civil Rights Division of the United States Department of Justice. He served in Mississippi and Alabama. Among many acts of immense courage, he stood with John Doar in Jackson in June 1963, when Doar talked down the angry black protesters headed for a brigade of white police officers in the aftermath of Medgar Evers's murder, thus preventing a bloodbath. Judge Henderson, an authentic champion of the civil rights movement, has been exceedingly kind and thoughtful and has counseled me socially, professionally, and in every way possible. Serving on this bench with him and my other colleagues has been the greatest honor of my life.

Willanna and Ben left Mississippi in 1965 and eventually settled in

Raleigh, North Carolina, with their three kids, Leah, Nicky, and Drew. There, in addition to being a mom of moms, Willanna enjoyed a rewarding career as a chief technical research librarian. For her part, after a transfer from MSCW, Sandy finished at MSU, obtained a master's degree and settled in Bellingham, Washington, with a career in social work. Sandy married in 1973 and eventually had four children, whom she wound up raising as a single mom.

After they retired, Willanna and Ben sold their suburban place and restored a vintage home in a leafy region of old Raleigh. In the spring of 2012, she began to lose weight, then learned she had pancreatic and liver cancer. She remained brave and upbeat. She savored the time she had left and remained immensely grateful for her life, especially for Ben and her devoted children and adoring grandchildren. She even found time to read and to improve a draft of this small work—and to encourage it. She died in August 2013. From the moment she established that little kindergarten on our porch, Willanna shone as the guiding light in our family—its moral compass. Sandy and I and our families gathered with Willanna's family in

Willanna (1958)

Raleigh in late 2013 for a memorial service. Ron was there, too. His memoriam brought burning tears to our eyes.

As for my pals at Provine High School, Junior Feild earned a doctorate in industrial psychology, then devoted himself to a career as a professor in the Harbert College of Business at Auburn University, retiring in 2015. Every Saturday morning for many years, we have talked by shortwave amateur radio (he's N4CLT; I'm N6XMW). Junior and Claire have now been married for a half century. They have a son, Taylor, a tropical botanist, with three young kids.

After Millsaps College and a PhD, then teaching (history), Ron Goodbread became a lawyer, a federal public defender in Washington, then a federal magistrate judge on the District of Columbia Superior Court. He retired to Leesburg, Virginia, with his third wife, Kay, to immerse himself in finishing a career-long project, a history of Reconstruction in Mississippi.

After the billboard project, Ann Smith Willoughby went on to the University of Southern Mississippi, then to Kansas City, where she founded the Willoughby Design Group, a graphic arts firm of national reputation, and raised a son and a daughter as a single mom.

Joe Turnage (with his partner Danny Cupit) had the best win-loss record in our final year on the debate team. But Joe preferred science to law and went on to become a nuclear engineer with a doctorate from MIT. He remains a leader in the large-scale power-generation industry and is semiretired now in San Juan Capistrano with his second wife, Angela. Together, they have three boys. He still loves Vegas.

Houston drew two of us. Sidney Craft became a renowned orthodontist there. He has loved three wives and two daughters, both now moms. Sidney has made many hikes with me in the Sierra. So has Walter Dowdle, who went on to become a petroleum engineer and to found his own firm in Houston. His wife (Marty Batt, also from Jackson), has been with him for fifty-plus years. They have three children, all now parents themselves. In 2016, MSU recognized Walter as the engineering alum of the year.

After Jack Purvis served as a combat helicopter pilot in Vietnam, he eventually became a colonel in the Mississippi National Guard before pursuing another career with the Mississippi Research and Development

Center, then yet another as an IT professional in a Jackson law firm. He and Anita (from Georgia) met while Jack was in the Army. They have three children, now grown, all MSU graduates. Jack and Anita live just outside Jackson, with a second home near MSU, both being huge MSU fans. He's made some Sierra backpacking trips and volunteers each winter as a ranch hand at our forty-acre place near Yosemite.

Our son John has also been blessed with much attention, care, and guidance from Walter, Sidney, Jack, and Junior. This has come via our annual Sierra backpacks and expeditions, well-attended by our Mississippi pals, that began in 1983 and have continued to this day. In his teens, John even spent a week with Walter and his wife Marty in Houston, and they have maintained their own special friendship. They have all been cherished aunts and uncles to John. I'd be jealous if I did not love them so much.

Carl Dicks served his country well and true as a gunner's mate in the Navy. Carl never married. He never wanted to. He lived his life very much the way he said he would—in the Navy. He didn't say it often, but Carl was proud of the way his pals turned out, just as we were of him. "Not so fucking bad," he would have said, "for some chickenshit kids on the wrong goddamn side of town in the poorest hellhole state in the Union." He died in 2006 from cigarettes. Carl happens to be buried within yards of my parents and brother.

Joe Posey went to Georgia Tech and then to MIT, earning a doctorate, an had a stellar career with NASA. He and his second wife, Dee Ann, have a son, Carter, who looks exactly like Joe did. Frank Whittington earned a doctorate and, like Junior, had a full career as a professor. Frank now teaches at George Mason University and has no plans to retire (our own Dorian Gray). Bennett Price got a law degree, moved to Alabama, married a friend of my sister Sandy (another small-world story), and quit law practice to run his wife's family business.

As for friends at MSU, many became lawyers. Coach Brad Bishop became the assistant dean at Samford University's Cumberland School of Law in Birmingham, a city where he also still serves as a municipal judge. Brad and Anne are still together and have two kids, long since adults, both with children of their own. Kirk Shaw became an artillery officer and then went to law school at the University of Virginia. During the following thirty years, he became a prized defense lawyer in employment cases in Mobile. He and Linda have been married for more than fifty years. They raised two sons. Kirk retired in 2012.

Scott Wendelsdorf followed me as president of the YMCA, then went on to law school at the University of Kentucky, and today remains in his dream job—Federal Public Defender for the United States District Court of the Western District of Kentucky. He and Maggie divorced. After a second marriage that ended in separation, Scott now gives all to the job he loves.

Cermette Clardy completed his service in Vietnam as an army intelligence officer and settled in South Carolina, where he has since retired with Anne after decades of running a consulting business.

Susan Eiland stayed on at MSU to earn a master's in literature, married a classmate, settled near Sacramento, and raised a daughter, Clare, now an artist.

Debbie Davis followed Scott as YMCA president, our first woman president, then earned a master's from Columbia University and a doctorate from Texas A&M, where her husband taught marine geophysics and Debbie counseled students. They are now retired to a tiny mountain village in Colorado.

Camilla Wilson returned from working as a Red Cross volunteer journalist in 1968 and returned to Vietnam to cover the war as a journalist for another year. When she returned to the States, she became an investigative reporter in Ohio and Minnesota and now teaches journalism at Minnesota State University Moorhead. Her daughter Leigh externed for me in 2014.

After a long career as an emergency room doctor in Birmingham, Dr. Richard Holmes returned to MSU in 2003 to serve as a staff doctor at the school infirmary. By then, 20 percent of the MSU student body was African American.

Danny Cupit was the only one among us to devote his entire life and career to Mississippi. He eventually left Dixon's practice and succeeded famously on his own in Jackson, specializing in civil rights and labor litigation on the plaintiff's side. For many years, he has practiced out of his offices on a corner facing the Mississippi capitol in a beautifully redone Victorian, "Galloway House," once visited by President Theodore

Roosevelt (Danny has a picture to prove it) on the same Mississippi visit that launched the "Teddy Bear."* Danny and Sharon have lived in Jackson for nearly fifty years, choosing not to flee to the white suburbs. They have been exceedingly generous in gifts to MSU. One large gift led to a first-class locker room for the men's basketball team at Humphrey Coliseum, a locker room they adorned with murals telling the story of the 1963 MSU team that defied the racist system to play in the NCAA tournament.

Danny and his career have embodied the spirit of Atticus Finch, a selfless devotion to making his hometown a more compassionate, a more generous, and a more just place to live.

Danny Cupit outside his Victorian law office (2016)

---

* Locals took the president hunting in the woods near Vicksburg, but no game appeared, so the sponsors let loose a captured bear cub for Roosevelt to shoot. He raised his rifle, paused, then lowered it, saying he just couldn't do it. The story captured the heart of America. Soon, "Teddy Bears" became the rage.

43

Conclusion

It is easier now to criticize the Mississippi of our youth. One reason it is easier is that since then, good people like Dixon Pyles, Betty Tucker, and Aaron Henry have devoted their life's work, and others like Medgar Evers and Vernon Dahmer have given their very lives, to make the place they loved better and more tolerant. Danny and Sharon carry on there still, ever deserving of—but always shrinking from—recognition for their lifelong contributions. Thanks to them and those like them, the danger in dissent is past. The main roadway on the MSU campus is now named for Dr. Martin Luther King Jr., and a major roadway in Jackson now honors Medgar Evers. A highway in Neshoba County where the three civil rights workers were murdered in 1964 now bears their names. Mississippi, like America, has become a different place. A better place.

But back then it was not so easy to criticize Mississippi—if you lived there. An anthem of the era asked, "Which side are you on, son? Which side are you on?" It became a soul-piercing question. Back then, even some homegrown white kids found it within themselves, by fits and turns, to ask that question, to stand up for something important, to stand against an evil system, to be on the side of justice and equality, and to hazard the consequences.

In the flower of youth, those moments trembled with meaning and electricity. Now, they repose in sepia—mere footnotes in the history of a turbulent and momentous struggle. Against the vast canvas of the epic events of that era, the tableau of a few white kids coming of age in Mississippi warrants but muted pastels, not the vivid hues due those authentic civil rights paladins who at huge personal risk dedicated themselves to the cause. Yet in those pastels is a story of how white America, even white kids in Missisippi, heard that anthem, asked which side they were on, embraced the idea of equality, and were won over to the right side of history.